Table of Contents

I. Introduction
   1. Outcomes & Indicators 2
   2. Stories 6
   3. Songs 10
   4. Games & Activities 11
   5. Crafts 21

II. Signs
   1. Character 24
   2. Emotions 71
   3. Greetings 97
   4. Manners 107

III. Handouts 117

IV. Index 124

Copyright © 2008 Time to Sign, Inc.

Outcomes & Indicators

The Child Outcomes and indicators are depicted as follows:

Domain
> Domain Element
>> Indicators

A. Language Development

A.1 Listening & Understanding

- A.1.a. Sign language naturally demonstrates increased ability to understand and participate in conversations, stories, songs, rhythms, and games
- A.1.b. Sign language assists in the understanding and following of simple and multiple-step directions
- A.1.c. Sign language greatly increases children's receptive vocabulary
- A.1.d. Sign language assists non-English-speaking children in learning to listen to and understand English as well sign language

A.2 Speaking & Communication

- A.2.a. Sign language assists in developing increasing abilities to understand and use sign language and English to communicate information, experiences, ideas, feelings, opinions, needs, and questions for other purposes
- A.2.b. Sign language instruction teaches children the use of an increasingly complex and varied signed and spoken vocabulary
- A.2.c. Sign language assists non-English speaking children in signing and speaking English

B. Literacy

B.1 Phonological Awareness

As teachers say and sign words together it serves as another way for children to understand and remember both the sign and the spoken word. When taught together sign instruction assists in providing the following benefits.

- B.1.a. Progresses in recognizing matching sounds in familiar words, songs, rhythms, games, stories, and other activities
- B.1.b. Associates sounds with written and signed words
- B.1.c. Children's use of sign language enhances language acquisition
- B.1.d. Children's learning of sign language simultaneously with words assist in like word differentiation of emergent readers

B.2 Book Knowledge & Appreciation

- B.2.a. Signing is an enjoyable activity for children that greatly enhances vocabulary, which makes learning to read easier and sometimes earlier
- B.2.b. Children who are taught sign language demonstrate progress in abilities

Character

to retell, using sign words, stories from books and personal experiences

B.2.c. Children who are taught sign language demonstrate progress in abilities to act out stories in dramatic play which is a natural extension of the hand and finger movements learned in sign language

B.3 Print Awareness and Concepts

B.3.a. Children who learn to sign develop a growing understanding of the different functions of forms of print such as signs, letters, and numbers

B.3.b. When written words are presented with the verbal and sign introduction/instruction children better learn to recognize a word as a unit of print

B.4 Early Writing

B.4.a. Begins to represent stories and experiences through signs, pictures, songs, games, and in play

B.5 Alphabet Knowledge

B.5.a. Shows progress in associating the names of letters with their signs, shapes, and sounds

B.5.b. Identifies all the letters of the alphabet, especially those in their own name

B.5.c. Knows that the letters of the alphabet are a special category of visual graphics that can be individually signed and named

C. Mathematics

C.1 Number & Operations

C.1.a. Children are taught the sign language counterparts to the numbers

C.1.b. Children count numbers to assist with the retention of the number they have reached

C.1.c. Signing assists with children's ability to count beyond the number 10

C.1.d. Signing assists with children's learning to make use of one-to-one correspondence in counting objects and matching numbers of groups of objects

C.2 Geometry & Spatial Sense

C.2.a. Signing assists with the recognition and ability to describe common shapes as shape signs accurately represent common shapes such as square, triangle, or circle

C.2.b Signing assists children in developing visual and spatial awareness

D. Science

D.1 Scientific Skills & Methods

D.1.a. Signing assists children in the understanding of scientific principles such as

Copyright © 2008 Time to Sign, Inc.

being able to express differences (such as big/little, open/closed, and more/less)
- D.1.b. Signing assists in increasing children's awareness
- D.1.c. Singing assists in the growing awareness of ideas and language related to time

D.2 Scientific Knowledge

- D.2.a. Signing assists in increasing awareness and beginning understanding of changes in material and cause-effect relationships
- D.2.b. Signing assists in increasing awareness of ideas and language related to time and temperature
- D.2.c. Signing assists in expanding knowledge of and respect for their body and the environment
- D.2.d. Signing enhances children's abilities to observe, describe and discuss the natural world, materials, living things, and natural processes

E. Creative Arts

E.1 Music
E.1.a. As children sign to music they develop increased interest and enjoyment in listening, singing, signing, finger plays, games, and performances

E.2 Movement
E.2.a. Children express through sign what is felt and heard in music

E.3 Dramatic Play
E.3.a. Children express themselves dramatically through signing

F. Social & Development

F.1 Self Concept
- F.1.a. Begins to develop and express awareness of self in terms of specific abilities, characteristics and preferences through the use of signing, for example they learn to sign their name and are given a sign name they feel reflects their personality
- F.1.b. Children's successful use of sign language enhances their confidence and self-esteem

F.2 Self Control
- F.2.a. Through the use of sign language children learn to express their feelings, emotions, needs, and opinions in everyday and in difficult situations without harming themselves, others, or property
- F.2.b. Through the use of sign language children demonstrate increased capacity to follows rules and routines, and to use materials purposefully, safely and respectfully
- F.2.c. Children's use of sign language raises communication awareness, enabling

Character

them to better tell and understand how their actions and words effect others

- F.2.d. Children's and teacher's use of sign language lowers children's noise levels in the classroom enhancing the learning atmosphere
- F.2.e. Children's use of sign language teaches them to pay better attention, they need to pay attention visually, rather than just listen
- F.2.f. Children's use of sign language increase their use of manners, which can help to eliminate potential misbehavior reactions
- F.2.g Children's use of sign language fosters an atmosphere in which children ask questions before acting, for example asking if their classmate is done with the toy before taking it and angering their classmate
- F.2.h. Classroom usage of sign language engages the teachers to be present with the child, they need to be making regular eye contact and can better see in the faces of children if anything is wrong, the child is unhappy, etc.

F.3 Cooperation

- F.3.a. Children's use of sign language increases their abilities to sustain interactions with peers through the use of manners, enabling them to express their feelings and emotions, by helping, and by sharing
- F.3.b. Children's use of sign language increases their abilities to use compromise and discussion in playing and resolving conflicts with classmates
- F.3.c. Children's use of sign language increases their abilities to give and take in interactions; to take turns in games or using materials; and to be participatory in activities while not being overly aggressive

F.4 Social Relationships

- F.4.a. Children's use of sign language increases their signing and speaking with and accepting guidance and directions from a wide range of familiar adults
- F.4.b. Children and teacher's use of sign language in the classroom enables all in the classroom to develop friendships with peers, this is particularly true and key for any special needs members of the class.
- F.4.c. Children's use of sign language teaches them to be especially aware when classmates are in need, upset, hurt, or angry; and in expressing empathy for others

F.5 Knowledge of Families & Communities

- F.5.a. The Young Children's Signing Program incorporates family signs to assist in children's understanding of family composition
- F.5.b. The Young Children's Signing Program incorporates gender signs, boy and girl, to assist in children's understanding of genders

G. Approaches to Learning

G.1 Initiative & Curiosity

- G.1.a. Children's use of sign language increases participation in an increasing variety of tasks and activities
- G.1.b. Children's use of sign language enhances their use of imagination and inventiveness in participation in tasks and activities

G.2 Engagement & Persistence

- G.2.a Children's learning of sign language also assist them as they increase their capacity to maintain concentration over time on a task, question, or set of directions or interactions

G.3 Reasoning & Problem Solving

- G.3.a. Children's learning and use of sign language assists in the recognition and problem solving through active exploration, including trial and error, and interactions and discussions with classmates and adults

H. Physical Health & Development

H.1. Fine Motor Skills

- H.1 a. Children's learning of sign language develops hand and arm strength and dexterity needed to control such instruments as a hammer, scissors, tape, and a stapler
- H.1.b. Children's learning of sign language develops hand-eye coordination required for use of building blocks, putting puzzles together, reproducing shapes and patterns, stringing beads, and using scissors
- H.1.c. Children's learning of sign language develops drawing and art tools such as pencils, crayons, markers, chalk, paint brushes, and computers
- H.1.d. Children's learning of sign language enables them to be able to pick up small objects

H.2 Gross Motor Skills

- H.2.a. Children's learning of sign language coordinates movements in throwing, catching, and bouncing balls

H.3 Health Status & Practices

- H.3.a. Children's learning of sign language enhances their ability to communicate health and hygiene problems to adults
- H.3.b. Children's learning of sign language enhances their knowledge of health and hygiene

Stories

<u>Arnie and the New Kid</u> by Nancy Carlson (feelings)
Topical signs to be learned: feelings, happy, sad, angry, new, friends, kid (child).
Indicators: A.1.a, A.1.b, A.1.c, A.1.d, A.2.a, A.2.b, A.2.c, B.1.a, B.1.b, B.1.c, B.1.d, B.2.a, B.2.b, B.2.c, B.3.a, B.3.b, B.4.a, C.2.b, F.1.b, F.2.a, F.2.c, F.2.d, F.2.e, F.2.h, G.1.a, G.1.b, G.2.a, H.1.a, H.1.b.

<u>Baby Faces</u> (DK Publishing)
Topical signs to be learned: happy, sad, puzzled, surprised, where's baby, peek-a-

Character

boo, angry, worried, crying, laughing, hungry, kiss, dirty, clean, tired, fast asleep.
Indicators: A.1.a, A.1.b, A.1.c, A.1.d, A.2.a, A.2.b, A.2.c, B.1.a, B.1.b,
B.1.c, B.1.d, B.2.a, B.2.b, B.2.c, B.3.a, B.3.b, B.4.a, C.2.b, F.1.b, F.2.a,
F.2.c, F.2.d, F.2.e, F.2.h, G.1.a, G.1.b, G.2.a, H.1.a, H.1.b.

Can I Help? By S. Harold Collins (helpfulness)
Topical signs to be learned: can, I, help, how, you, feel, sick, dizzy, confused, hurt,
okay, where, you, go, lost, have, questions, know, little bit, sign language, try, this,
emergency, need, accident, danger, police, fire truck, interpreter, me, telephone,
number, address, don't be afraid, wait, here, lie down, sit, come, with, me, move,
finished, here, soon, when, where, hurt, doctor, nurse, hospital, ambulance.
Indicators: A.1.a, A.1.b, A.1.c, A.1.d, A.2.a, A.2.b, A.2.c, B.1.a, B.1.b,
B.1.c, B.1.d, B.2.a, B.2.b, B.3.a, B.3.b, B.4.a, C.2.b, F.1.b, F.2.a, F.2.c,
F.2.d, F.2.e, F.2.f, F.2.h, , G.1.a, G.1.b,G.2.a, G.3.a, H.1.a, H.1.b.

The Children's Manners Book by Alida Allison (manners)
Topical signs to be learned: children, please, thank you, excuse
me, manners, share, may I, sorry, welcome.
Indicators: A.1.a, A.1.b, A.1.c, A.1.d, A.2.a, A.2.b, A.2.c, B.1.a, B.1.b,
B.1.c, B.1.d, B.2.a, B.2.b, B.3.a, B.3.b, B.4.a, C.2.b, F.1.b, F.2.a, F.2.c,
F.2.d, F.2.e, F.2.f, F.2.h, , G.1.a, G.1.b,G.2.a, H.1.a, H.1.b.

Cookies: Bite-Size life Lessons by Amy Krouse Rosenthal (character)
Topical signs to be learned: cooperate, you, I, patient, wait, cookies, finish, still, more,
minute, nice, proud, like, modest/humble, tell, make, best, respect, give, first, grandmother,
trustworthy, hold, go, come, fair, share, compassionate, worry, take, all, generous, awful,
still, have, half, excuse me, please, give, thank you, honest, tell, courageous, not, easy,
mine, loyal, friend, open-minded, try, content, sit, wise/wisdom, think, know, all, little.
Indicators: A.1.a, A.1.b, A.1.c, A.1.d, A.2.a, A.2.b, A.2.c, B.1.a, B.1.b,
B.1.c, B.1.d, B.2.a, B.2.b, B.3.a, B.3.b, B.4.a, C.2.b, F.1.b, F.2.a, F.2.c,
F.2.d, F.2.e, F.2.f, F.2.h, , G.1.a, G.1.b,G.2.a, H.1.a, H.1.b.

A Day's Work By Eve Bunting (honesty, hard work)
Topical signs to be learned: grandfather, cold, hot, bring, kid, school, mother,
father, tall, skinny/thin, jacket/coat, food, flower, new, house, weed, hat, thank
you, nice, day, good, work, proud, eat, drink, water, beautiful, garden, know,
ask, tomorrow, Sunday, take, finish, more, important, teach, home.
Indicators: A.1.a, A.1.b, A.1.c, A.1.d, A.2.a, A.2.b, A.2.c, B.1.a, B.1.b, B.1.c,
B.1.d, B.2.a, B.2.b, B.2.c, B.3.a, B.3.b, B.4.a, C.2.b, F.1.b, F.2.a, F.2.c,
F.2.d, F.2.e, F.2.h, F.5.a, G.1.a, G.1.b, G.2.a, G.3.a, H.1.a, H.1.b.

Hello! Good-bye! by Aliki
Topical signs to be learned: hello, goodbye, all, use, word, meet, go, begin, end,
welcome, good morning, guess, good evening, none, hug, kiss, sign, bow, look, like/
same, peace, love, music, funny, quiet, wonderful, happy, sad, travel/journey,
other, language, good night, short, long, not, easy, hard, hurt, sun, moon.
Indicators: A.1.a, A.1.b, A.1.c, A.1.d, A.2.a, A.2.b, A.2.c, B.1.a, B.1.b,
B.1.c, B.1.d, B.2.a, B.2.b, B.2.c, B.3.a, B.3.b, B.4.a, C.2.b, F.1.b, F.2.a,
F.2.c, F.2.d, F.2.e, F.2.h, G.1.a, G.1.b, G.2.a, H.1.a, H.1.b.

Character

<u>I Feel</u> by George Ancoma (feelings)
Topical signs to be learned: feelings, happy, sad, angry.
Indicators: A.1.a, A.1.b, A.1.c, A.1.d, A.2.a, A.2.b, A.2.c, B.1.a, B.1.b,
B.1.c, B.1.d, B.2.a, B.2.b, B.2.c, B.3.a, B.3.b, B.4.a, C.2.b, F.1.b, F.2.a,
F.2.c, F.2.d, F.2.e, F.2.h, G.1.a, G.1.b, G.2.a, H.1.a, H.1.b.

<u>Inside of Me I Have Feelings</u> by Nancy Lee Walker (feelings)
Topical signs to be learned: feelings, happy, sad, angry, inside, me.
Indicators: A.1.a, A.1.b, A.1.c, A.1.d, A.2.a, A.2.b, A.2.c, B.1.a, B.1.b,
B.1.c, B.1.d, B.2.a, B.2.b, B.2.c, B.3.a, B.3.b, B.4.a, C.2.b, F.1.b, F.2.a,
F.2.c, F.2.d, F.2.e, F.2.h, G.1.a, G.1.b, G.2.a, H.1.a, H.1.b.

<u>Inside of Me If I Feel</u> by Nancy Lee Walker (feelings)
Topical signs to be learned: feel, happy, sad, angry, inside, me.
Indicators: A.1.a, A.1.b, A.1.c, A.1.d, A.2.a, A.2.b, A.2.c, B.1.a, B.1.b,
B.1.c, B.1.d, B.2.a, B.2.b, B.2.c, B.3.a, B.3.b, B.4.a, C.2.b, F.1.b, F.2.a,
F.2.c, F.2.d, F.2.e, F.2.h, G.1.a, G.1.b, G.2.a, H.1.a, H.1.b.

<u>I'm Sorry</u> by Gina & Mercer Mayer (Manners)
Topical signs to be learned: sorry, sister, bicycle, walk, jump, rope, brother, blanket, dirty, playing, outside, hide-and-seek, curtain, favorite, book, baby, mother, please, quietly, bedroom, window, ball, garden, forgot, rained, washed, pants, new, shoes, bunny, top, off, ant, farm, dinner, broccoli, bath, bathroom, dollhouse, little, more, careful.
Indicators: A.1.a, A.1.b, A.1.c, A.1.d, A.2.a, A.2.b, A.2.c, B.1.a, B.1.b,
B.1.c, B.1.d, B.2.a, B.2.b, B.3.a, B.3.b, B.4.a, C.2.b, F.1.b, F.2.a,
F.2.d, F.2.e, F.2.g, F.2.h, G.1.a, G.1.b, G.2.a, H.1.a, H.1.b.

<u>It's Mine!</u> by Leo Lionni (manners)
Topical signs to be learned: three, frogs, all, day, mine, water, off, ground/dirt, jump, catch, butterfly, hear, shout, peace, worm, for, thunder, rain, afraid, rock, disappear/dissolve, one, cold, feel, better, together, share, stop, safe, happy, beautiful, ours.
Indicators: A.1.a, A.1.b, A.1.c, A.1.d, A.2.a, A.2.b, A.2.c, B.1.a, B.1.b,
B.1.c, B.1.d, B.2.a, B.2.b, B.3.a, B.3.b, B.4.a, C.2.b, F.1.b, F.2.a, F.2.c,
F.2.d, F.2.e, F.2.g, F.2.h, G.1.a, G.1.b, G.2.a, H.1.a, H.1.b.

<u>It's Mine</u> by Gina & Mercer Mayer (Manners)
Topical signs to be learned: baby, brother, sleep, my, bear, no, mine, mom, share, eat, popsicle, please, train, sister, play, reading, favorite, book, hide, book, drinking, cup, outside, sandbox, inside, blocks, dinosaur, rabbit, blow, bubbles, drop, blanket, doll, big, frog,
Indicators: A.1.a, A.1.b, A.1.c, A.1.d, A.2.a, A.2.b, A.2.c, B.1.a, B.1.b,
B.1.c, B.1.d, B.2.a, B.2.b, B.3.a, B.3.b, B.4.a, C.2.b, F.1.b, F.2.a, F.2.c,
F.2.d, F.2.e, F.2.g, F.2.h, G.1.a, G.1.b, G.2.a, H.1.a, H.1.b.

<u>The Little Old Lady Who Was Not Afraid of Anything</u> by Linda Williams
Topical signs to be learned: little, old, lady, not, afraid, windy, afternoon, house, walk, forest, long, far, dark, moon, home, stop, two, big, shoes, move, behind, hear, pants, shirt, white, black, hat, fast, near, orange, pumpkin, head, ran, inside,

Copyright © 2008 Time to Sign, Inc.

Character

safe, sit, quiet, idea, good night, morning, window, look, garden, bird, away.
Indicators: A.1.a, A.1.b, A.1.c, A.1.d, A.2.a, A.2.b, A.2.c, B.1.a, B.1.b, B.1.c, B.1.d, B.2.a, B.2.b, B.2.c, B.3.a, B.3.b, B.4.a, C.2.b, F.1.b, F.2.a, F.2.c, F.2.d, F.2.e, F.2.h, G.1.a, G.1.b, G.2.a, H.1.a, H.1.b.

<u>Manners Can Be Fun</u> by Munro Leaf (manners)
Topical signs to be learned: fun, please, thank you, excuse me, manners, share, may I, sorry, welcome.
Indicators: A.1.a, A.1.b, A.1.c, A.1.d, A.2.a, A.2.b, A.2.c, B.1.a, B.1.b, B.1.c, B.1.d, B.2.a, B.2.b, B.3.a, B.3.b, B.4.a, C.2.b, F.1.b, F.2.a, F.2.c, F.2.d, F.2.e, F.2.f, F.2.h, , G.1.a, G.1.b,G.2.a, H.1.a, H.1.b.

<u>Miss Spider's Tea Party</u> by David Kirk (manners)
Topical signs to be learned: please, thank you, manners, share, may I, welcome.
Indicators: A.1.a, A.1.b, A.1.c, A.1.d, A.2.a, A.2.b, A.2.c, B.1.a, B.1.b, B.1.c, B.1.d, B.2.a, B.2.b, B.3.a, B.3.b, B.4.a, C.2.b, F.1.b, F.2.a, F.2.c, F.2.d, F.2.e, F.2.f, F.2.h, , G.1.a, G.1.b,G.2.a, H.1.a, H.1.b.

<u>On Monday When It Rains</u> by Cherryl Kachenmeister (feelings)
Topical signs to be learned: feelings, happy, sad, angry, Monday, rain.
Indicators: A.1.a, A.1.b, A.1.c, A.1.d, A.2.a, A.2.b, A.2.c, B.1.a, B.1.b, B.1.c, B.1.d, B.2.a, B.2.b, B.2.c, B.3.a, B.3.b, B.4.a, C.2.b, F.1.b, F.2.a, F.2.c, F.2.d, F.2.e, F.2.h, G.1.a, G.1.b, G.2.a, H.1.a, H.1.b.

<u>Perfect Pigs</u> by Marc Brown and Stephan Krensky (manners)
Topical signs to be learned: pigs, please, thank you, excuse me, manners, share, may I, sorry, welcome.
Indicators: A.1.a, A.1.b, A.1.c, A.1.d, A.2.a, A.2.b, A.2.c, B.1.a, B.1.b, B.1.c, B.1.d, B.2.a, B.2.b, B.3.a, B.3.b, B.4.a, C.2.b, F.1.b, F.2.a, F.2.c, F.2.d, F.2.e, F.2.f, F.2.h, , G.1.a, G.1.b,G.2.a, H.1.a, H.1.b.

<u>Say Please</u> by Virginia Austin (Manners)
Topical signs to be learned: dog, throw, ball, please, ducks, may I have some, bread, cat, milk, thank you, pig, scratch, back, favorite, book, read
Indicators: A.1.a, A.1.b, A.1.c, A.1.d, A.2.a, A.2.b, A.2.c, B.1.a, B.1.b, B.1.c, B.1.d, B.2.a, B.2.b, B.3.a, B.3.b, B.4.a, C.2.b, F.1.b, F.2.a, F.2.c, F.2.d, F.2.e, F.2.f, F.2.h, , G.1.a, G.1.b,G.2.a, H.1.a, H.1.b.

<u>Someday We'll Have Very Good Manners</u> by Harriet Ziefert (Manners)
Topical signs to be learned: grow up, good, manners, polite, please, thank you, telephone, say, remember, wipe (clean), feet, knock, patiently, line, temper, take turns, seat, door, open, table (eating), napkin, knife, fork, excuse me, finished, proud, mine, shout, interrupt, presents, now, kids.
Indicators: A.1.a, A.1.b, A.1.c, A.1.d, A.2.a, A.2.b, A.2.c, B.1.a, B.1.b, B.1.c, B.1.d, B.2.a, B.2.b, B.3.a, B.3.b, B.4.a, F.1.b, F.2.a, F.2.c, F.2.e, F.2.f, F.2.g, F.2.h, G.1.a, G.1.b,G.2.a, H.1.a, H.1.b.

<u>Those Mean Nasty Dirty Downright Disgusting but…Invisible Germs</u> by Judith Anne Rice (illness manners) Topical signs to be learned: cold, sick, mouth, nose, tissue.

Indicators: A.1.a, A.1.b, A.1.c, A.1.d, A.2.a, A.2.b, A.2.c, B.1.a, B.1.b, B.1.c, B.1.d, B.2.a, B.2.b, B.3.a, B.3.b, B.4.a, C.2.b, F.1.b, F.2.a, F.2.c, F.2.d, F.2.e, F.2.f, F.2.h, , G.1.a, G.1.b,G.2.a, H.1.a, H.1.b, H.3.a, H.3.b.

Today I Feel Silly And Other Moods That Make My Day by Jamie Lee Curtis (emotions)
Topical signs to be learned: silly, mood, bad, grumpy, mean, angry, today, feelings, hurt, joyful, confused, glad, quiet, understands, cried, excited, cranky, lonely, happy, great, discouraged, frustrated, sad, frown, face, great, best, inside, ok, "How do you feel Today?"
Indicators: A.1.a, A.1.b, A.1.c, A.1.d, A.2.a, A.2.b, A.2.c, B.1.a, B.1.b, B.1.c, B.1.d, B.2.a, B.2.b, B.2.c, B.3.a, B.3.b, B.4.a, C.2.b, F.1.b, F.2.a, F.2.c, F.2.d, F.2.e, F.2.h, G.1.a, G.1.b, G.2.a, H.1.a, H.1.b.

What Do You Do, Dear by Sesyle Joslin (manners)
Topical signs to be learned: please, thank you, excuse me, manners, share, may I, sorry, welcome.
Indicators: A.1.a, A.1.b, A.1.c, A.1.d, A.2.a, A.2.b, A.2.c, B.1.a, B.1.b, B.1.c, B.1.d, B.2.a, B.2.b, B.3.a, B.3.b, B.4.a, C.2.b, F.1.b, F.2.a, F.2.c, F.2.d, F.2.e, F.2.f, F.2.h, , G.1.a, G.1.b,G.2.a, H.1.a, H.1.b.

Why Does That Man Have Such A Big Nose? by Mary Beth Quinsey (manners)
Topical signs to be learned: please, thank you, excuse me, manners, share, may I, sorry, welcome.
Indicators: A.1.a, A.1.b, A.1.c, A.1.d, A.2.a, A.2.b, A.2.c, B.1.a, B.1.b, B.1.c, B.1.d, B.2.a, B.2.b, B.3.a, B.3.b, B.4.a, C.2.b, F.1.b, F.2.a, F.2.c, F.2.d, F.2.e, F.2.f, F.2.h, , G.1.a, G.1.b,G.2.a, H.1.a, H.1.b.

Songs

If You're Happy And You Know It (emotions)
Indicators: A.1.a, A.1.b, A.1.c, A.1.d, A.2.a, A.2.b, A.2.c, B.1.a, B.1.c, B.1.d, B.2.a, B.2.b, B.3.a, B.4.a, C.2.b, E.1.a, E.2.a, F.1.b, F.2.a, F.2.b, F.2.e, F.2.h, F.3.c, G.1.a, G.1.b, H.1.a, H.1.b, H.1.d.

Make New Friends – (friends)
Indicators: A.1.a, A.1.b, A.1.c, A.1.d, A.2.a, A.2.b, A.2.c, B.1.a, B.1.c, B.1.d, B.2.a, B.2.b, B.3.a, B.4.a, C.2.b, E.1.a, E.2.a, F.1.b, F.2.e, F.2.h, F.3.c, F.4.b, G.1.a, G.1.b, H.1.a, H.1.b, H.1.d

More We Sign Together, The (friends)
Indicators: A.1.a, A.1.b, A.1.c, A.1.d, A.2.a, A.2.b, A.2.c, B.1.a, B.1.c, B.1.d, B.2.a, B.2.b, B.3.a, B.4.a, C.2.b, E.1.a, E.2.a, F.1.b, F.2.e, F.2.h, F.3.c, F.4.b, G.1.a, G.1.b, H.1.a, H.1.b, H.1.d

Please and Thank You - (manners)
Indicators: A.1.a, A.1.b, A.1.c, A.1.d, A.2.a, A.2.b, A.2.c, B.1.a, B.1.c, B.1.d, B.2.a, B.2.b, B.3.a, B.4.a, C.2.b, E.1.a, E.2.a, F.1.b, F.2.e, F.2.f, F.2.h, F.3.c, G.1.a, G.1.b, H.1.a, H.1.b, H.1.d

Tell Me Why (emotions)
Indicators: A.1.a, A.1.b, A.1.c, A.1.d, A.2.a, A.2.b, A.2.c, B.1.a, B.1.c,

Character

B.1.d, B.2.a, B.2.b, B.3.a, B.4.a, C.2.b, E.1.a, E.2.a, F.1.b, F.2.a, F.2.b, F.2.e, F.2.h, F.3.c, G.1.a, G.1.b, H.1.a, H.1.b, H.1.d

Ten Little Amigos (numerals and sets, friends)
Indicators: A.1.a, A.1.b, A.1.c, A.1.d, A.2.a, A.2.b, A.2.c, B.1.a, B.1.c, B.1.d, B.2.a, B.2.b, B.3.a, B.4.a, C.1.a, C.1.b, C.1.d, C.2.b, E.1.a, E.2.a, F.1.b, F.2.e, F.2.h, F.3.c, F.4.b, G.1.a, G.1.b, H.1.a, H.1.b, H.1.d

Use Your Manners - (manners)
Indicators: A.1.a, A.1.b, A.1.c, A.1.d, A.2.a, A.2.b, A.2.c, B.1.a, B.1.c, B.1.d, B.2.a, B.2.b, B.3.a, B.4.a, C.2.b, E.1.a, E.2.a, F.1.b, F.2.e, F.2.f, F.2.h, F.3.c, G.1.a, G.1.b, H.1.a, H.1.b, H.1.d

Way Up High in the Apple Tree (foods, colors, emotions)
Indicators: A.1.a, A.1.b, A.1.c, A.1.d, A.2.a, A.2.b, A.2.c, B.1.a, B.1.c, B.1.d, B.2.a, B.2.b, B.3.a, B.4.a, C.2.b, E.1.a, E.2.a, F.1.a, F.1.b, F.2.e, F.2.h, F.3.c, G.1.a, G.1.b, H.1.a, H.1.b, H.1.d

You are My Sunshine (emotions)
Indicators: A.1.a, A.1.b, A.1.c, A.1.d, A.2.a, A.2.b, A.2.c, B.1.a, B.1.c, B.1.d, B.2.a, B.2.b, B.3.a, B.4.a, C.2.b, E.1.a, E.2.a, F.1.b, F.2.a, F.2.b, F.2.e, F.2.h, F.3.c, G.1.a, G.1.b, H.1.a, H.1.b, H.1.d.

Games & Activities

Blowing Bubbles (gentleness)
Outdoor activity if at all possible. Have each of the children pair up with a container of bubbles. Have them teach each other how to fingerspell their names. Have one of the children blowing the bubbles while their partner tries to catch them. Have the teacher use a large bubble wand to produce great big bubbles for the children to try to catch.

Topical signs to be learned: bubbles, fingerspelling.
Indicators: A.1.a, A.1.b, A.1.c, A.1.d, A.2.a, A.2.b, A.2.c, B.1.c, B.2.a, B.2.b, B.2.c, C.2.b, F.1.b, F.2.a, F.2.b, F.2.c, F.2.d, F.2.e, F.2.h, F.3.a, F.3.b, F.3.c, F.3.b, F.3.c, F.4.b, G.1.a, G.1.b, G.2.a, G.3.a, H.1.a, H.1.b, H.1.d.

Bubbles (gentleness)
Materials: clean pail, 1 cup dish washing detergent (Joy or Dawn work best), 3-4 T. glycerin from pharmacy (optional), 10 cups clean cold water, large spoon, plastic bubble wands.

Pour the water into the pail and add the liquid detergent and the glycerin. (Glycerin makes the bubbles more durable.) Lightly stir and skim off any froth with a spoon. Give a plastic wand to each child and demonstrate how to blow bubbles. Using a bowl placed in the water table reduces the amount of spills and cleanup, as well as frustration when children accidentally spill their bubbles. Set up a bubble obstacle course in the classroom where the children blow bubbles as they walk along a path. The path could include such exercises as blowing a

Copyright © 2008 Time to Sign, Inc.

bubble through a hula hoop, walk backwards, catching bubbles, and so forth. You can also purchase a giant bubble wand for outdoor play.

Topical signs to be learned: bubbles, blow, water, gentle.
Indicators: A.1.a, A.1.b, A.1.c, A.1.d, A.2.a, A.2.b, A.2.c, B.1.c, B.2.a, B.2.b, B.2.c, C.2.b, F.1.b, F.2.a, F.2.b, F.2.c, F.2.d, F.2.e, F.2.h, F.3.a, F.3.b, F.3.c, F.3.b, F.3.c, F.4.b, G.1.a, G.1.b, G.2.a, G.3.a, H.1.a, H.1.b, H.1.d.

Co-operation Playdough

Materials: 2/3 cup salt, 2 cups flour, 1/3 cup vegetable oil, 2/3 cup water, few drops of food coloring, large bowl, large spoon (for each group making dough).

Divide class into groups of 3-6. Discuss turn taking asking what it means and when we take turns. After talking about the importance of taking turns, tell the class that they are going to make play dough but they have to take turns when making it. Allow the children to take turns adding, mixing, and stirring the ingredients together. (Mix dry ingredients first and then add oil, water, and food coloring). When finished, divide dough into parts and give to children to play with.
Be sure to reinforce turn taking during other activities and try to plan other activities where children can practice turn taking (snack, games, sharing time, etc.).

Topical signs to be learned: turn/take turn, bowl, spoon,
water, share, please, thank you, next.
Indicators: A.1.a, A.1.b, A.1.c, A.1.d, A.2.a, A.2.b, A.2.c, B.1.c, B.2.a, B.2.b, B.2.c, C.2.b, F.1.b, F.2.b, F.2.c, F.2.d, F.2.e, F.2.f, F.2.h, F.3.a, F.3.b, F.3.c, F.3.b, F.3.c, F.4.b, F.4.c, G.1.a, G.1.b, G.2.a, G.3.a, H.1.a, H.1.b, H.1.d.

Dancing Balloons (friendship)

Materials: 9-inch round balloons, permanent markers, large
sheets of colored tissue paper, masking tape, music.

Give each child a blown-up balloon. Have the children make faces on the balloons using permanent markers. Make a body out of the tissue paper. Using masking tape, attach one corner of the paper to the balloon knot, wrapping the tape around it several times. While music plays, the children can dance with their new dance partner by throwing the balloons in the air and catching them or laying the balloons across their extended arms and revolving around and around. They can change partners by changing balloons.

Topical signs to be learned: dance, friend, balloon, music, face.
Indicators: A.1.a, A.1.b, A.1.c, A.1.d, A.2.a, A.2.b, A.2.c, B.1.c, B.2.a, B.2.b, B.2.c, C.2.b, F.1.b, F.2.b, F.2.c, F.2.d, F.2.e, F.2.h, F.3.a, F.3.b, F.3.c, F.4.b, G.1.a, G.1.b, G.2.a, G.3.a, H.1.a, H.1.b, H.1.d.

Emotions Game

Circle game. Teach the children the different emotions signs. Once they are familiar with the signs, read or make up statements that would refer to one of the emotions. Have the children do the sign for the emotion.

Character

Examples:
I dropped my ice cream. I got a new toy. I got a boo boo.

After you, the teacher, go through a few examples have the children think of an emotion to sign and then have them develop a sentence/statement using the word/sign.

Topical signs to be learned: emotion signs, I, etc.
Indicators: A.1.a, A.1.b, A.1.c, A.1.d, A.2.a, A.2.b, A.2.c, B.1.c, B.2.a, B.2.b, B.2.c, C.2.b, E.3.a, F.1.b, F.2.a, F.2.b, F.2.d, F.2.e, F.2.h, F.3.a, F.3.c, F.4.b, G.1.a, G.1.b, G.2.a, G.3.a, H.1.b, H.1.d.

Face Pass (fine & performing arts, emotions)
This game has 2-20 players
Go over the emotion signs. The players are arranged in a close circle, They can be seated, if desired. The leader starts by making a funny, dramatic, or unusual face, and then the leader passes this face to the next person, who must copy the face. Both then turn to show everyone else in the group the faces made. The second person then creates a new face to pass to a third person, following the same direction. This continues around the circle until everyone has a turn. It's amazing what people will come up with, and even more so when a very serious person comes up with the most ridiculous face. If someone is having trouble coming up with a face to pass, let them know that they can say and sign "Next," with the option to make a face at the end if they wish. This will prevent embarrassment about participating in the game. On the other hand, you can encourage (not force) them to try, because it is great fun. Doing something quickly without thinking is probably the best way to cope. Talk about different emotions some of the faces represented and use the signs for those emotions.

Topical signs to be learned: leader, face, funny, show, next, emotion signs.
Indicators: A.1.a, A.1.b, A.1.c, A.1.d, A.2.a, A.2.b, A.2.c, B.1.c, B.2.a, B.2.b, B.2.c, C.2.b, F.1.b, F.2.a, F.2.b, F.2.e, F.2.h, F.3.a, F.3.c, F.4.b, G.1.a, G.1.b, G.2.a, G.3.a, H.1.b, H.1.d.

Feather Face Painting (gentleness)
Pair up the children. Have them sit directly in front of one another. Have them teach their sign fingerspelled names to their partners. Explain that they are going to take turns painting their partners faces with feathers (do not include the eyes). First the eyebrows, then the forehead, then the hair, then the cheeks, then the nose, then the lips, then the chin and finally the neck. Be sure you emphasize painting softly. There are no actual paints involved with this activity.

Topical signs to be learned: Face, nose, mouth, colors, feather, paint.
Indicators: A.1.a, A.1.b, A.1.c, A.1.d, A.2.a, A.2.b, A.2.c, B.1.c, B.2.a, B.2.b, B.2.c, C.2.b, F.1.b, F.2.a, F.2.b, F.2.c, F.2.d, F.2.e, F.2.h, F.3.a, F.3.b, F.3.c, F.3.b, F.3.c, F.4.b, G.1.a, G.1.b, G.2.a, G.3.a, H.1.a, H.1.b, H.1.d.

Feather Play (gentleness)
Materials: small, brightly colored feathers; other materials depend on the activity.

- Fill an empty water table with feathers for sensory experience.

Copyright © 2008 Time to Sign, Inc.

- Take one feather of each color and tape each onto a separate paper plate. Hide the remaining feathers and tell the children to find them. Have them sort the feathers according to color by putting each feather on the matching plate.
- Give each child one small feather. Play soft music. Have the children toss their feathers in the air and try to catch them.
- Play "Find Big Bird" by having the children close their eyes while you place a trail of feathers leading to a picture or stuffed toy of Sesame Street's Big Bird.

Topical signs to be learned: feather, gentle, play, find, color signs, separate, music, catch.
Indicators: A.1.a, A.1.b, A.1.c, A.1.d, A.2.a, A.2.b, A.2.c, B.1.c, B.2.a, B.2.b, B.2.c, C.2.b, F.1.b, F.2.a, F.2.b, F.2.c, F.2.d, F.2.e, F.2.f, F.2.h, F.3.a, F.3.b, F.3.c, F.3.b, F.3.c, F.4.b, G.1.a, G.1.b, G.2.a, G.3.a, H.1.a, H.1.b, H.1.d.

Feeling Faces (feelings, emergencies)
Materials: paper, markers/pencils/crayons, scissors.

Cut out blank faces that the children can fill in for themselves. Discuss different feelings, while teaching them the signs for those words. Have them fill in the faces for the last week as to how they felt each day or fill one out each day(overall).

Topical signs to be learned: afraid, angry, calm, excited, feelings, grumpy, happy, hurt, sad, silly, scared, sorry, surprised, tired, upset.
Indicators: A.1.a, A.1.b, A.1.c, A.1.d, A.2.a, A.2.b, A.2.c, B.1.c, B.2.a, B.2.b, B.2.c, C.2.b, F.1.b, F.2.b, F.2.c, F.2.d, F.2.e, F.2.h, F.2.a, F.2.b, F.2.c, F.3.a, F.3.c, F.4.c, G.1.a, G.1.b, G.2.a, G.3.a, H.1.b, H.1.d.

Feelings Felt Board – (emotions)
Make a simple felt body with a face. The body should look similar to that of a gingerbread man. Make several circular faces that fit the body. Each face should portray a different feeling. Put the body and all the faces on the felt board. Have the children come up one at a time to choose the appropriate face for the emotion signed. Have the child tell when/why they had similar feelings. Have all the children form each of the signed emotions together as a group.

Topical signs to be learned: body, face, emotion signs.
Indicators: A.1.a, A.1.b, A.1.c, A.1.d, A.2.a, A.2.b, A.2.c, B.1.c, B.2.a, B.2.b, B.2.c, C.2.b, E.3.a, F.1.b, F.2.a, F.2.b, F.2.d, F.2.e, F.2.h, F.3.a, F.3.c, F.4.b, G.1.a, G.1.b, G.2.a, G.3.a, H.1.b, H.1.d.

Feelings Lotto (emotions)
Materials: paper, marker, clean contact paper, construction paper.

Draw six circles on a piece of paper. Draw a happy face, sad face, angry face, afraid face, silly face, and surprised face and label each with the emotion (or other emotions, if desired). Make one copy for each child. There are three different things you can do with the faces:
1. Leave some sheets whole, cut up others to make a Lotto game.
2. Cut out pairs of each feeling, mount them on construction paper, laminate or cover with clear contact paper, and use them to play concentration.

Copyright © 2008 Time to Sign, Inc.

Character

    3. Use the page as a tool to help children clarify how they feel. The teacher can ask "Which face looks like how you feel?" and then have them circle and color that faces. Discuss.

Topical signs to be learned: emotion signs, face, which, how, you, circle.
Indicators: A.1.a, A.1.b, A.1.c, A.1.d, A.2.a, A.2.b, A.2.c, B.1.c, B.2.a, B.2.b, B.2.c, C.2.b, E.3.a, F.1.b, F.2.a, F.2.b, F.2.d, F.2.e, F.2.h, F.3.a, F.3.c, F.4.b, G.1.a, G.1.b, G.2.a, G.3.a, H.1.b, H.1.d.

Firefly Game (friendship)

Form a circle and turn down the room lights. Let one child pretend to be the firefly by holding the flashlight. The firefly shines the flashlight around and stops the beam on another child and recites (while the rest of the group signs):

    Firefly, firefly, oh so bright!
    Firefly, firefly shines at night
    Firefly, firefly, what a sight!
    I see _____ in the night!

The firefly has to fingerspell the name of the child they spotlighted and the child becomes the next firefly and we begin again until everyone has had a turn to be the firefly.

Topical signs to be learned: feather, gentle, bowl, firefly, bright, night, sight/see, name.
Indicators: A.1.a, A.1.b, A.1.c, A.1.d, A.2.a, A.2.b, A.2.c, B.1.c, B.2.a, B.2.b, B.2.c, B.4.a, B.5.b, B.5.c, C.2.b, F.1.b, F.2.b, F.2.c, F.2.d, F.2.e, F.2.h, F.3.c, F.4.b, G.1.a, G.1.b, G.2.a, G.3.a, H.1.a, H.1.b, H.1.d.

Fishing for Friends (friendship)

Materials: Polaroid camera or pictures of each child from home, scissors, metal lid, stick, string, magnet, wash tub or other large container (optional).

Take a Polaroid picture of each of the members of class or have them bring in a picture from home (good time to do this after school pictures come out). Glue each picture to a lid. Have the children sit in a circle and sign their names one at a time so that all can see how they are spelled/fingerspelled. Spread the pictures out on the floor or have a large washtub. Have each of the children take turns fishing (with a pole that has a magnet tied to it) for a classmate. The person then gives the fishing pole to the person who they picked. Have the children return the "fish" they have caught. Once the children have played 10 rounds or so as a single group, then pass out a few more fishing poles to speed along the fun. Add the extra poles by picking those who do not seem to be getting picked by the other children.

Topical signs to be learned: fish, friends, fingerspelling of names, pick, catch.
Indicators: A.1.a, A.1.b, A.1.c, A.1.d, A.2.a, A.2.b, A.2.c, B.1.c, B.2.a, B.2.b, B.2.c, B.5.b, B.5.c, C.2.b, F.1.b, F.2.b, F.2.c, F.2.d, F.2.e, F.2.h, F.3.c, F.4.b, G.1.a, G.1.b, G.2.a, G.3.a, H.1.a, H.1.b, H.1.d.

Friendship Map (friendship)

Materials: butcher paper, map, crayons, markers, or colored pencils; toy cars, trucks and figures.

Copyright © 2008 Time to Sign, Inc.

Have the children sit around a very large piece of paper (roll or butcher block). Show them a real map and how it is used. Have them each fingerspell their name for the whole group to see. Then ask them each to draw a house in front of were they are sitting, on the paper. Have each of the children take turns drawing a line (road) from their house to that of a friend. They need to fingerspell the name of their friend. Label each of the roads for the child that drew them. Let them play with and add more features to their map. They can play with cars, trucks, figures, etc. Post on the wall when they are done or roll up for them to play with on another day.

Topical signs to be learned: house, friends, road, fingerspelling of names, draw, car.
Indicators: A.1.a, A.1.b, A.1.c, A.1.d, A.2.a, A.2.b, A.2.c, B.1.c, B.2.a, B.2.b, B.2.c, B.5.b, B.5.c, C.2.b, F.1.b, F.2.b, F.2.c, F.2.d, F.2.e, F.2.h, F.3.c, F.4.b, G.1.a, G.1.b, G.2.a, G.3.a, H.1.a, H.1.b, H.1.c, H.1.d.

The Great Predictor (self-control, behavior)
Materials: costume turban (or one made from wrapping a towel around the head) with a large feather plume.

The children take a turn at being "The Great Predictor," that is, they wear the turban and answer questions the teacher asks. Each questions begins with "Oh, Great Predictor..." and then follows with a question designed to get the children thinking about consequences and rewards for their actions. Be sure to have questions relevant to the classroom/child. Here are some sample questions:
What will happen if we get upset and hit or push someone?
What will happen if we share?
What will happen if we interrupt others?
What will happen if we leave our toys or things out?

Topical signs to be learned: ask, what, happen, we, signs in questions asked.
Indicators: A.1.a, A.1.b, A.1.c, A.1.d, A.2.a, A.2.b, A.2.c, B.1.c, B.2.a, B.2.b, B.2.c, C.2.b, F.1.b, F.2.a, F.2.b, F.2.c, F.2.d, F.2.e, F.2.f, F.2.h, F.3.a, F.3.b, F.3.c, F.3.b, F.3.c, F.4.b, F.4.c, G.1.a, G.1.b, G.2.a, G.3.a, H.1.a, H.1.b, H.1.d.

Hug A Bug (friendship)
Materials: music and music player.

Play fun dance music. When the music stops, the children find one of several others to hug until the music resumes, then they start dancing again.

Topical signs to be learned: music, stop, dance, hug, friend, gentle, go.
Indicators: A.1.a, A.1.b, A.1.c, A.1.d, A.2.a, A.2.b, A.2.c, B.1.c, B.2.a, B.2.b, B.2.c, C.2.b, E.2.a, E.3.a, F.1.b, F.2.b, F.2.c, F.2.d, F.2.e, F.2.h, F.3.c, F.4.b, G.1.a, G.1.b, G.2.a, G.3.a, H.2.a.

Let's Play Tea Party (manners, food)
Materials: tea set (child size or full adult size) including cups, saucers, spoons, teapot, sugar bowl, creamer pitcher; table and chairs, real or pretend tea, water, juice or other

Character

liquid; real or pretend cake, cookies, crackers, or small sandwiches; plates, napkins, table cloth and decorations (optional); stuffed animals or dolls as additional guests.

Prepare a small table for a tea party with enough chairs for each person or toy invited. Cover the table with a tablecloth, or set out place mats. Set out the tea set, napkins, plates, and whatever other items you might have for the tea party. One person is the host and the others are guests. The host is in charge of pouring tea and serving the guests (you can take turns on being the host). Use polite conversation and manner signs (thank you, more please, welcome, etc.).

Topical signs to be learned: manners, more, tea, table, chair, cup, teapot, saucer (plate), cookie, cake, sandwich, cracker, sugar, cream/milk.
Indicators: A.1.a, A.1.b, A.1.c, A.1.d, A.2.a, A.2.b, A.2.c, B.1.c, B.2.a, B.2.b, B.2.c, B.4.a, C.2.b, E.3.a, F.1.a, F.1.b, F.2.a, F.2.b, F.2.c, F.2.d, F.2.e, F.2.f, F.2.g, F.3.a, F.3.b, F.3.c, F.4.b, F.4.c, F.5.a, G.1.a, G.1.b, G.2.a, G.3.a, H.1.a, H.1.b, H.1.d, H.2.a.

Mad Hatter (conflict resolution)
Talk to your children about appropriate ways they can express their emotions when they are angry or unhappy. Teach them the signs for these emotions. Write down each of their answers on an index card. Draw or cut and paste a picture that represents their actions. Put all the cards into a hat. Explain that when they are angry or upset they can draw a card from the hat and do what it says or use their signs to express their signs in a positive manner. The Mad Hatter should be available during free play times.

Topical signs to be learned: emotion signs, hat, write, draw, picture, action, angry, upset, pick, do, say, sign, play, time.
Indicators: A.1.a, A.1.b, A.1.c, A.1.d, A.2.a, A.2.b, A.2.c, B.1.c, B.2.a, B.2.b, B.2.c, B.5.b, B.5.c, C.2.b, F.1.b, F.2.a, F.2.b, F.2.c, F.2.d, F.2.e, F.2.h, F.3.c, F.4.b, F.4.c, G.1.a, G.1.b, G.2.a, G.3.a, H.1.a, H.1.b, H.1.c, H.1.d.

Nonelimination Musical Chairs (cooperation, sharing)
Materials: chairs, tape or cd player, tape or cd.

Here is a twist on musical chairs. It is played like regular musical chairs with this slight modification: instead of elimination of players, the students must cooperate and share the available chairs to accommodate all the members of the class. As each chair is removed, the players must either sit on one another's laps or share chairs. It's an interesting activity both to be in and to watch.

Topical signs to be learned: chair, music, cooperate, share.
Indicators: A.1.a, A.1.b, A.1.c, A.1.d, A.2.a, A.2.b, A.2.c, B.1.c, B.2.a, B.2.b, B.2.c, C.2.b, F.1.b, F.2.a, F.2.b, F.2.c, F.2.d, F.2.e, F.2.h, F.3.a, F.3.b, F.3.c, F.4.b, G.1.a, G.1.b, G.2.a, G.3.a, H.1.b, H.1.d.

Polite or Impolite? (respect, manners)
Materials: three teddy bears.

Explain the definitions of polite and impolite. Emphasize courtesy and following

Copyright © 2008 Time to Sign, Inc.

the Golden Rule. Set up a table with three teddy bears. Explain that the bears are having tea and a snack. Ask them to raise their hands and tell you if they are being polite or impolite. Give enough examples that you can call on all the children.

Examples:
How are you today?
Hello.
Give me some cookies!
Pass the cookies please.
Thank you for inviting me.
May I have some sugar please?
Give me the sugar!
Wiping her hand on her shirt (motion).
May I have a napkin please?
Tell me the time!
What time is it?
Give me some more tea!
May I have some more tea please?
Get it yourself!
I would be happy to pass you the tea.
Please join us next time.
Thank you, everything was wonderful.
You should have bought more cookies!

Topical signs to be learned: manners, hello, please, thank you, welcome, may I, excuse me, pass, teddy bear.
Indicators: A.1.a, A.1.b, A.1.c, A.1.d, A.2.a, A.2.b, A.2.c, B.1.c, B.2.a, B.2.b, B.2.c, C.2.b, F.1.b, F.2.a, F.2.b, F.2.c, F.2.d, F.2.e, F.2.f, F.2.h, F.3.a, F.3.b, F.3.c, F.4.b, F.4.c, G.1.a, G.1.b, G.2.a, G.3.a, H.1.b, H.1.d.

Relaxing Images (visualization)

Talk to the children about seeing things with their eyes closed (visualizing). Can you see when you dream? What sorts of things do you see? Can you hear or taste or touch or feel anything? Have the children sit in a circle. Tell them to lie down and close their eyes. Ask them to picture in their minds the detailed common item you describe.

1. I see something round and white. It is too high for me to touch. It is brightest in the night. It can change shapes from a sliver to full circle. It can effect the tides here on earth. The moon.
2. I see something red. It is sort of round and can be eaten. It grows on a vine, rather than a tree. I eat it in my salad. A tomato.
3. I see something green. It is cold blooded and scaly. It has four legs and can walk on land, as well as swim in water. It has a tremendous tail. It has a long snout and lots of teeth. An alligator.
4. I see something metallic and shiny. It has many keys, but no doors to open. It can remember whatever I tell it and it can teach me a lot. I also play games with it and chat with people from far away places. A computer.

When you are through with each item, tell the children to open their eyes and ask them each to sign the key words as they describe what they pictured in their heads.

Character

Topical signs to be learned: colors, objects, descriptive words.
Indicators: A.1.a, A.1.b, A.1.c, A.1.d, A.2.a, A.2.b, A.2.c, B.1.c, B.2.a, B.2.b, B.2.c, C.2.b, F.1.b, F.2.a, F.2.b, F.2.c, F.2.d, F.2.e, F.2.h, F.3.a, F.3.b, F.3.c, F.4.b, G.1.a, G.1.b, G.2.a, G.3.a, H.1.b, H.1.d.

Respect Mother Earth (respect, science & nature)
Materials: trash bags, recyclable items, gloves.

Have the children label bags of various items that can be recycled (plastic, glass, bags, aluminum, newspapers, etc.). Talk about other items that they can recycle (batteries, tires, etc.). Have the children sort through a couple bags of items to fill the bags they labeled. Check the bags with the children as they sit in a circle and talk about some of the different items that are made recycled material. What effect does this have on the earth? Have the children wear gloves and collect trash nearby. Have them sort it into their bags. Put the rest in the trash. Talk about what happens to the trash (off to the landfill, some items may degrade in months or years, while others will never degrade). What effect does this have on the earth?

Topical signs to be learned: recycle, bag, earth.
Indicators: A.1.a, A.1.b, A.1.c, A.1.d, A.2.a, A.2.b, A.2.c, B.1.c, B.2.a, B.2.b, B.2.c, C.2.b, D.1.b, D.2.c, F.1.b, F.2.a, F.2.b, F.2.c, F.2.d, F.2.e, F.2.h, F.3.a, F.3.b, F.3.c, F.4.b, G.1.a, G.1.b, G.2.a, G.3.a, H.1.b, H.1.d.

Say Something Nice
Materials: soft ball that is easy to catch (such as Nerf or foam ball).

Have everyone sit in a circle. Then either throw, pass, or roll a Nerf ball to someone else in the circle and give that person a compliment. No repeats to persons are allowed until everyone has had the ball and a compliment. Ask the group to try to give different compliments each time. That's it! It feels good for someone to acknowledge you!

Topical signs to be learned: ball, sit in circle, throw, roll, say, nice, feel, good.
Indicators: A.1.a, A.1.b, A.1.c, A.1.d, A.2.a, A.2.b, A.2.c, B.1.c, B.2.a, B.2.b, B.2.c, C.2.b, F.1.b, F.2.a, F.2.b, F.2.c, F.2.d, F.2.e, F.2.f, F.2.h, F.3.a, F.3.b, F.3.c, F.4.b, F.4.c, G.1.a, G.1.b, G.2.a, G.3.a, H.1.b, H.1.d.

Star Message
Materials: paper, scissors, small sticky stars, pen, glass jar.

Cut 1" paper squares for each child. Place a stick star on one side of each paper. Print a star message on the other side. Suggested star messages: be a friend to everyone; be kind; be polite; help others if they need it; and use nice words. Fold up the paper squares and place them in the glass jar.

Discuss what it means to be a star! A star is someone who is special. If you are a star, everyone wants to be your friend. People smile when they see you. You are liked for the wonderful things that you can do and the wonderful person you are! Display the star jar. The star jar will help find out different ways to be stars in the classroom. One child chooses a star message. Read each message and give an example for each one.

Copyright © 2008 Time to Sign, Inc.

Or you can have students come up with their own star messages and then share them with the class.

Topical signs to be learned: character signs, manners signs, star, friend, special, pick.
Indicators: A.1.a, A.1.b, A.1.c, A.1.d, A.2.a, A.2.b, A.2.c, B.1.c, B.2.a, B.2.b, B.2.c, C.2.b, F.1.b, F.2.a, F.2.b, F.2.c, F.2.d, F.2.e, F.2.f, F.2.h, F.3.a, F.3.b, F.3.c, F.4.b, G.1.a, G.1.b, G.2.a, G.3.a, H.1.b, H.1.d.

The Talking Wand (listening)
Materials: wand or toy microphone.

Discuss with the class that it is impolite to interrupt while someone else is talking. To help remember that, only the person who has raised their hand and is holding the wand (or microphone) may talk. That way, everyone can hear and understand what is being said and can practice being good listeners.

Topical signs to be learned: polite/manners, talk, remember, listen, practice, good.
Indicators: A.1.a, A.1.b, A.1.c, A.1.d, A.2.a, A.2.b, A.2.c, B.1.c, B.2.a, B.2.b, B.2.c, C.2.b, F.1.b, F.2.a, F.2.b, F.2.c, F.2.d, F.2.e, F.2.f, F.2.h, F.3.a, F.3.b, F.3.c, F.4.a, F.4.b, F.4.c, G.1.a, G.1.b, G.2.a, G.3.a, H.1.b, H.1.d.

Toilet Paper Pull
Materials: colored or patterned toilet paper.

On each table place a roll of colored or patterned toilet paper. Without being told why, the group is instructed to pass the roll around, and each person may take as much as he wishes from the roll. When every person has taken from the roll, they are told they must tell one fact or interesting piece of information about themselves for each square they have torn off. For some, this may mean only one or two things—some may have to relate 25!

Topical signs to be learned: toilet, paper, take, tell, information, about, you, every.
Indicators: A.1.a, A.1.b, A.1.c, A.1.d, A.2.a, A.2.b, A.2.c, B.1.c, B.2.a, B.2.b, B.2.c, C.2.b, F.1.a, F.1.b, F.2.a, F.2.b, F.2.c, F.2.d, F.2.e, F.2.f, F.2.h, F.3.a, F.3.b, F.3.c, F.4.b, G.1.a, G.1.b, G.2.a, G.3.a, H.1.b, H.1.d.

Trash Sort (responsibility, respect, community)
Materials: empty, clean, plastic, glass, and metal containers; newspapers, grocery bags, markers, work gloves, trash bags.

Label each grocery bag with an appropriate picture or name to identify the type of items to be placed in the bag. Place all the items on a table and all the children to sort them into the correct bags.

Wear work gloves and collect litter on a neighborhood walk.
Sort the items after returning to the classroom.

Topical signs to be learned: empty, clean, dirty, use, bag, sort, type.
Indicators: A.1.a, A.1.b, A.1.c, A.1.d, A.2.a, A.2.b, A.2.c, B.1.c, B.2.a, B.2.b,

Character

B.2.c, C.2.b, D.1.b, D.2.c, F.1.b, F.2.a, F.2.b, F.2.c, F.2.d, F.2.e, F.2.h, F.3.a, F.3.b, F.3.c, F.4.b, G.1.a, G.1.b, G.2.a, G.3.a, H.1.b, H.1.d.

Who Feels Happy At School Today? – (emotions)
Who feels happy at school today?
All who do clap your hands this way (clap).
Who feels happy at school today?
All who do wink your eyes this way (wink).
Who feels happy at school today?
All who do jump in the air this way (jump).

Topical signs to be learned: who, feel, happy, school., today, all, clap, eyes, jump.
Indicators: A.1.a, A.1.b, A.1.c, A.1.d, A.2.a, A.2.b, A.2.c, B.1.c, B.2.a, B.2.b, B.2.c, C.2.b, F.1.a, F.1.b, F.2.a, F.2.b, F.2.c, F.2.d, F.2.e, F.2.f, F.2.h, F.3.a, F.3.b, F.3.c, F.4.b, G.1.a, G.1.b, G.2.a, G.3.a, H.1.b, H.1.d.

You're Not Listening (respect)
Often there is a strong correlation between respecting others and listening to what they have to say. As we listen we show those speaking that what they have to say matters and that we care about them. Listening is also key to learning. Use the following suggested ideas to enhance the listening skills of your children:
1. Sign instructions as often as possible, save your voice. You can sign transitions, instructions, commands, compliments, answers to questions, etc. as a part of your daily routine with the children. This is particularly effective with children who typically cannot remain quite or sit still and listen. They are learning to hear with there eyes. This can even help ADHD/hyperactive children to be better able to pay attention and learn.
2. Tell/sign or read/sign a story while underneath a parachute.
3. In a darkened corner or room have one of the children hold a flashlight upon you as you sign along to a book or story.
4. Use props to compliment story/signing time. Puppets, stuffed animals, toys, etc. help to keep your activity exciting and help to keep their attention.

Set up a play campfire and tent. Tell/sign camping stories. Sing/sign camping signs.
Indicators: A.1.a, A.1.b, A.1.c, A.1.d, A.2.a, A.2.b, A.2.c, B.1.c, B.2.a, B.2.b, B.2.c, C.2.b, F.1.a, F.1.b, F.2.a, F.2.b, F.2.c, F.2.d, F.2.e, F.2.f, F.2.h, F.3.a, F.3.b, F.3.c, F.4.a, F.4.b, F.4.c, G.1.a, G.1.b, G.2.a, G.3.a, H.1.b, H.1.d.

Crafts

Balloon Friends (friendship)
Materials: 8-9 Inch round balloons, cardboard, yarn, colored construction paper, scissors, glue, markers.

Talk about what makes friends special. Then cut out the feet of the friend they are making on the cardboard. Cut a slit into the center of the feet and insert the knot on the bottom of the balloon. Children can make and decorate the faces as they see fit.

Copyright © 2008 Time to Sign, Inc.

Topical signs to be learned: balloon, friend, colors, scissors, glue, face.
Indicators: A.1.b, A.1.c, A.1.d, A.2.a, A.2.b, A.2.c, B.1.c, B.2.a, C.2.b, F.1.b, F.2.a, F.2.b, F.2.c, F.2.d, F.2.e, F.2.h, F.3.c, F.4.a., F.4.b, G.1.a, G.1.b, G.2.a, H.1.a, H.1.b, H.1.c, H.1.d.

Friendship Bracelet (friendship)
Materials: Baker's clay, small plastic straws (coffee), tempera paint, small brushes, string. (Baker's clay can be purchased or made by mixing 2 cups of flour, 1 cup of salt, adding water until it forms a dough consistency.)

Explain that the purpose behind the making of this bracelet is to put together as many beads from different friends in the classroom as they can. Have the children roll out small beads from the clay. Each child should make at least 10 beads. Poke a hole through the beads with the straw. Allow beads to dry for 2 days or more. Have the children paint the beads as they see fit. When the beads are dry have the children exchange beads with the other children. They should only have one of their own beads left. String the beads to form the bracelets.

Topical signs to be learned: friend, ball, paint, brushes, art, string.
Indicators: A.1.b, A.1.c, A.1.d, A.2.a, A.2.b, A.2.c, B.1.c, B.2.a, C.2.b, F.1.b, F.2.b, F.2.c, F.2.d, F.2.e, F.2.h, F.3.c, F.4.a., F.4.b, G.1.a, G.1.b, G.2.a, H.1.a, H.1.b, H.1.c, H.1.d.

Jewel Floats
Materials: large clear plastic bottles with caps, baby oil or water, food coloring (optional), waterproof tape or hot glue gun, old jewelry, glitter, scraps of foil, small plastic toys.

Have children work in small groups or individually. Fill the bottles with baby oil or water, add food coloring if desired. Have the children cut up foil scraps and drop them in the bottle. Add glitter, old jewelry, and small toys. Put the cap securely on the bottle and tape or glue it closed. While repeatedly turning the bottle upside down, the children can search for and track particular objects. Place the floats so that they are accessible to the children in the room. The jewel float is a relaxing and soothing toy.
You can make floats to fit any theme being studied (ocean, color theme, animals, etc.).

Topical signs to be learned: bottle, water, color signs, search/look for.
Indicators: A.1.b, A.1.c, A.1.d, A.2.a, A.2.b, A.2.c, B.1.c, B.2.a, C.2.b, F.1.b, F.2.a, F.2.b, F.2.c, F.2.d, F.2.e, F.2.h, F.3.c, F.4.a., G.1.a, G.1.b, G.2.a, H.1.a, H.1.b, H.1.c, H.1.d.

My Little Ocean (calming, gentleness)
Materials: 2-liter clear plastic bottles with caps, baby oil, water, food coloring, duct (or other waterproof) tape, small-medium size plastic jewels, glitter, strips of foil, small sea shells, sand, small plastic sea toys.

Begin by putting 1 part baby oil to 3 parts water. Then add food coloring, if desired. Then put in varying amounts of each materials inside the bottle (sand, sea shells, sea toys, glitter, strips of foil, jewels). Then put cap on tightly and tape with duct tape.

Topical signs to be learned: ocean, colors, sand, toys, see, calm, quiet.

Copyright © 2008 Time to Sign, Inc.

Character

Indicators: A.1.b, A.1.c, A.1.d, A.2.a, A.2.b, A.2.c, B.1.c, B.2.a, C.2.b, F.1.b, F.2.a, F.2.b, F.2.c, F.2.d, F.2.e, F.2.h, F.3.c, F.4.a., G.1.a, G.1.b, G.2.a, H.1.a, H.1.b, H.1.c, H.1.d.

Pussy Willow Pictures (gentleness, springtime, nature)

Materials: pussy willow branches, light blue construction paper, brown crayons, glue sticks, small cotton balls, gray finger paint (tempura), small bowls.

Have the children touch the pussy willow branches to see how soft they are. Begin by having the children draw the branches of the pussy willow on the light blue construction paper. Then have them glue on the cotton balls. Older children can use gray finger paint to paint the buds, instead of using cotton balls. Pour some of the paint into small bowls, just a little so as to barely cover the bottom. Have the children press down on the paint in the bowls with their index finger and them use their finger to make the bud on the picture. Repeat until you have enough buds.

Topical signs to be learned: paper, brown, glue, gray, paint, bowls, calm, quiet.
Indicators: A.1.b, A.1.c, A.1.d, A.2.a, A.2.b, A.2.c, B.1.c, B.2.a, C.2.b, F.1.b, F.2.a, F.2.b, F.2.c, F.2.d, F.2.e, F.2.h, F.3.c, F.4.a., G.1.a, G.1.b, G.2.a, H.1.a, H.1.b, H.1.c, H.1.d.

Sneeze Pictures (illness manners)

Materials: paper, glue, crayons or markers, facial tissue.

Discuss the importance of covering one's mouth when coughing or sneezing. Explain that when we cough or sneeze we can spread germs that can make others sick. Have the children draw and color a face (for young children a pre-drawn face to color is a good idea). When they have finished have them glue a piece of tissue paper to the nose to serve as a reminder of what to do when we cough or sneeze.

Topical signs to be learned: sick, color, face, manners, mouth, nose, paper, remember.
Indicators: A.1.b, A.1.c, A.1.d, A.2.a, A.2.b, A.2.c, B.1.c, B.2.a, C.2.b, F.1.b, F.2.a, F.2.b, F.2.c, F.2.d, F.2.e, F.2.h, F.3.c, F.4.a., G.1.a, G.1.b, G.2.a, H.1.a, H.1.b, H.1.c, H.1.d, H.3.a, H.3.b.

Character Signs

-

Senáles

De carácter

Character

25

Place both "C" handshapes around the wide-opened eyes with the thumbs hear each side of the nose, palms facing forward.

alert – alerta

Copyright © 2008 Time to Sign, Inc.

Character

Move both open hands from near each cheek, palms facing each other, straight forward simultaneously.

[Also: pay attention]

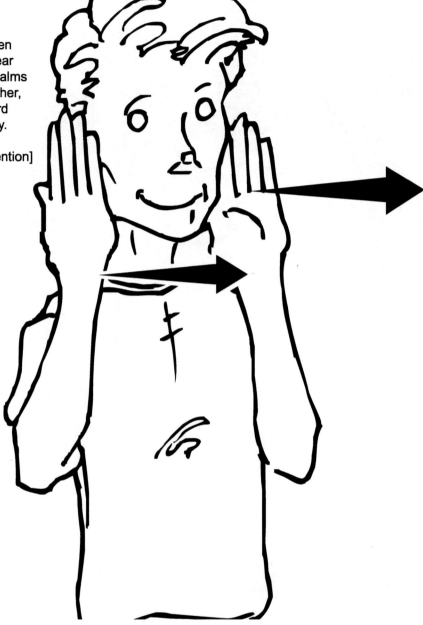

attentive – atento

Character

27

Move the bent middle fingertip of the dominant "5" handshape, across the back of the reference open hand from the wrist off the fingertips, palms facing down.

[Also: empty]

available – disponible

Copyright © 2008 Time to Sign, Inc.

28

Character

Move both "B" handshapes, palms facing up, from in front of the body forward simultaneously.

[Also: give]

benevolent– benévolo

Copyright © 2008 Time to Sign, Inc.

Character

Begin with the fingertips of both "5" handshapes on each shoulder, palms facing in and fingers pointing back, bring the hands deliberately forward while closing into "S" handshapes.

[Also: brave, confident]

bold - atrevido

Character

Tap the little finger side of the dominant "K" handshape with a double movement across the index finger side of the reference "K" handshape, palms facing in opposite directions.

[Also: careful]

cautious/discrete–
precavido/discreto

Character

Begin with the bent middle finger of the dominant "5" handshape pointing forward in front of the dominant shoulder, move the hand forward in repeated circular movement.

[Also: mercy, sympathy]

compassionate – compasivo

Copyright © 2008 Time to Sign, Inc.

Character

Begin with both "B" handshapes in front of the chest, dominant hand above the reference hand and both palms facing down, bring the index finger sides of both hands against the chest.

[Also: satisfied]

content – contento, satisfecho

Character  33

With the thumbs and index fingers of both "F" handshapes intersecting, move the hands in a flat circle in front of the chest.

[Also: unity]

cooperate – cooperar

Copyright © 2008 Time to Sign, Inc.

Character

Move the index finger side of the dominant "4" handshape, palm facing reference, from the forehead in an outward arc.

[Also: make-up, invent, create]

creative- creativo

Character

Move the extended dominant index finger from the dominant side of the forehead, palm facing reference, down in front of the chest while changing into an "F" handshape, ending with both "F" hands in front of the body, palms facing each other.

[Also: decide]

decisive – decidido

Copyright © 2008 Time to Sign, Inc.

Character

Begin with the index finger side of the dominant "R' handshape, palm facing reference, near the dominant side of the forehead, bring the hand downward and forward. Then with the dominant "10" handshape in front of the chest, palm facing down, twist the hand upward and to the dominant ending with palm facing up and the extended thumb pointing dominant. Next, move the dominant "O" handshape, palm facing reference in front of the forehead, toward the head with a double movement.

[Sign: respect + others + opinion]

deferent – deferente

Character

With the extended dominant index finger across the extended reference index finger, palms facing down, move both fingers down slightly with a double movement.

[Also: reliable]

dependable – confiable

Character

Begin with the extended thumb of the dominant open hand touching the dominant temple, palm facing forward and fingers pointing up, bend the fingers downward with a deliberate movement.

[Also: persistent]

determined – decidido

Copyright © 2008 Time to Sign, Inc.

Character  39

Bring the heel of the dominant "A" handshape, palm facing forward, in a double circular movement down across the back of the reference "S" handshape held in front of the chest.

[Also: work hard]

diligent – diligente

Character

Begin with the dominant "S" handshape near the dominant side of the forehead, palm facing reference, flick the index finger upward with a sudden movement.

[Also: comprehend, perceive, understand,

discern – dicernir

Character  41

Begin with the thumb of the dominant "10" handshape resting on the back of the reference "10" handshape thumb, both palms facing down, move the hands forward and down a short distance.

[Also: continual, constant, persistent, steadfast, steady]

endure – soportar, sobrellevar

Copyright © 2008 Time to Sign, Inc.

Character

Rub the palms of both open hands, palms facing each other, back and forth against each other with a double alternating movement.

[Also: aspire, eager, motivation, zeal]

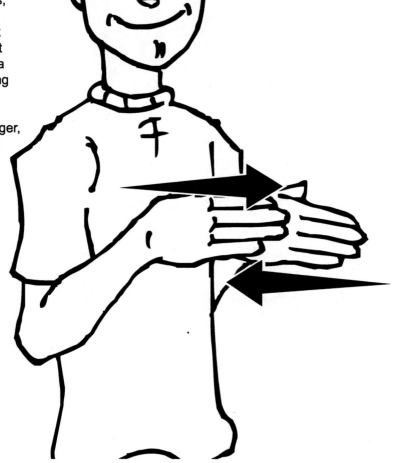

enthusiastic – entusiasmado

Character

43

With the little finger side of the dominant "1" handshape across the index finger side of the reference "1" handshape, palms facing in opposite directions, move the hands downward in front of the chest.

[Also: consistent, regular.]

faithful – fiel

Copyright © 2008 Time to Sign, Inc.

Character

Grasp the fingers of the reference open hand, palm facing dominant, with the fingers of the dominant flattened "O" handshape, and then bend the reference fingers downward until both palms are facing down and hands are bent.

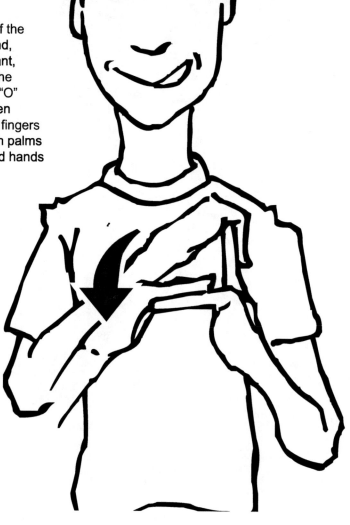

flexible - flexible

Character

Brush the fingertips of the dominant open hand, palm facing down, across the palm of the upturned reference open hand from the heel off the fingertips with a double movement.

[Also: excuse]

forgiving – perdonado, disculpando

46

Character

Begin with both curved "5" handshapes in front of each side of the chest, palms facing up, bring the hands down with a double movement while closing the fingers to the thumbs each time.

[Also: soft, tender]

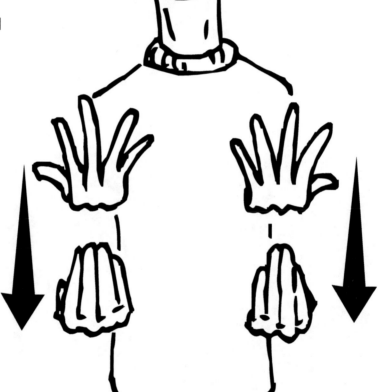

gentle – delicado, gentil

Copyright © 2008 Time to Sign, Inc.

Character

Begin with the dominant open hand near the mouth and the reference open hand somewhat forward, palms facing in and fingers pointing up, move both hands forward.

[Also: appreciative, thankful]

grateful– agradecido

Character

Begin with both "H" handshapes in front of the face, dominant hand higher than the reference hand and palms facing in opposite directions, bring both hands downward and forward in a slight arc.

[Also: honor]

honorable – honorable

Character

Bring the dominant open hand, palm facing in near the middle of the chest, in a forward circle around the back of the reference open hand, palm facing in, as it moves in a circle around the dominant hand.

[Also: generous, kind]

hospitable – hospitalario

Character

Bring the dominant "B" handshape, palm facing reference and fingers pointing up, from in front of the mouth downward and forward under the reference open hand held in front of the chest, palm facing down.

[Also: modest]

humble/meek – humilde

Character

Begin with both "5" handshapes in front of the body, palms facing up and fingers pointing forward, bring the hands back toward the chest while constricting the fingers toward the palms.

[Also: desire, passion, want]

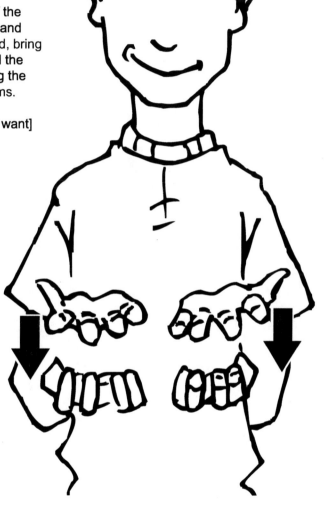

initiative - iniciativa

Character

Brush the fingers of the dominant open hand, palm facing in and fingers pointing reference, upward in a repeated circular movement on the chest.

[Also: cheerful, delighted, happy]

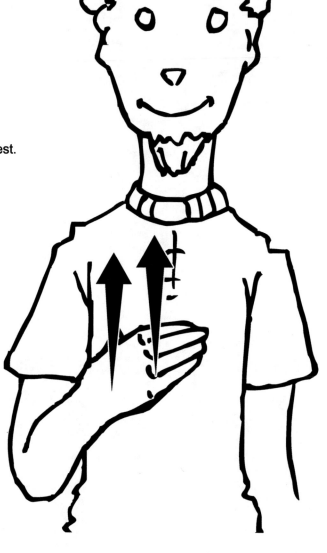

joyful – alegre

Character  53

Move both "F" handshapes, palms facing each other, up and down in front of each side of the chest with a repeated alternating movement.

[Also: judge, justice]

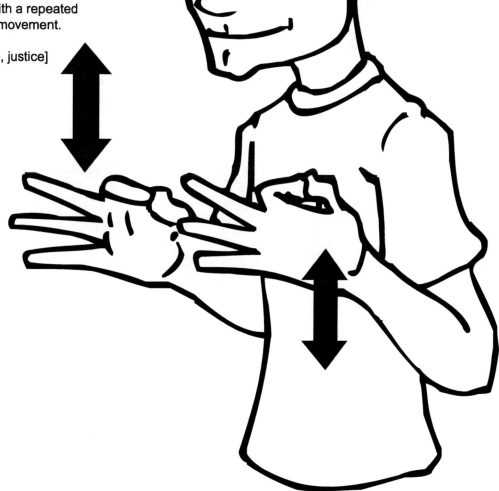

just – justo

Copyright © 2008 Time to Sign, Inc.

Character

Begin with the thumb of the dominant "L" handshape, palm facing reference, touching the forehead, move the dominant hand forward in an arc.

loyal - leal

Character

Begin with the dominant "O" handshape in front of the forehead and the reference "O" handshape in front of the reference shoulder, both palms facing in, bring the hands downward simultaneously while opening the fingers, ending with both open hands in front of the body, palms facing up and fingers pointing forward.

obedient – obediente

Character

Slide the extended fingers of the dominant "N" handshape, palm facing down, from the heel to the fingers of the upturned reference open hand, fingers pointing forward.

[Also: neat]

orderly - ordenado

Character

Move the dominant "A" handshape, palm facing reference, downward in front of the chin.

[Also: tolerate]

patient – paciente

Character

With both modified "X" handshapes in front of each side of the chest, palms facing each other and dominant hand closer to the chest than the reference hand, move the hands forward with a short double movement.

[Also: urge]

persuasive- persuasivo

Character

Begin with both extended index fingers pointing forward in front of the body, palms facing each other, pull the hands quickly back toward the chest while constricting the index fingers into "X" handshapes. Next bring the palm of the dominant open hand downward across the back of the reference open hand held in front of the body, both palms facing down. Then tap the index finger of the dominant "X" handshape, palm facing down, with a double movement on the wrist of the reference "S" handshape held across the body, palm facing down.

[Sign: fast + on + time]

[Also: prompt]

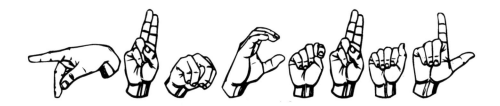

punctual – puntual

Move both "S" handshapes, palms facing down, downward simultaneously with a short double movement in front of each side of the body. Then bring the dominant "5" handshape upward from in front of the body while closing the thumb and index finger to form an "F" handshape. Next with both extended index fingers pointing up in front of the mouth, dominant hand behind the reference and palms facing forward, bend the wrists down simultaneously, ending with fingers pointing forward and the palms facing down.

[Sign: capable + find + answer]

resourceful – ingenioso

Character

61

Begin with the dominant "R" handshape, palm facing reference and fingers pointing up, near the dominant side of the forehead, bring the hand downward and forward.

respectful - respetuoso

Copyright © 2008 Time to Sign, Inc.

Tap the fingers of both "R" handshapes, palms facing in, on the shoulder with a double movement.

responsible – responsable

Character  63

Begin with both "S" handshapes crossed at the wrists in front of the chest, palms facing in opposite directions, twist the wrists and move the hands apart, ending with the hands in front of each shoulder, palms facing forward.

[Also: free, liberty, safe]

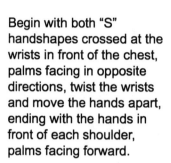

secure – seguro

Copyright © 2008 Time to Sign, Inc.

Character

Begin with the dominant "10" handshape held in front of the chest, palm facing reference, move forward from the wrist with a double movement. Then with both curved "5" handshapes on either side of the chest, palms facing in, bring the hands down while closing into "S" handshapes ending with palms facing up.

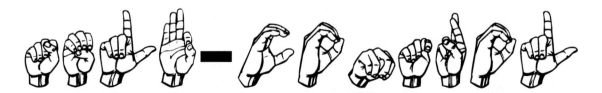

self-control – dominio de sí mismo

Character

Begin with the bent middle finger of the dominant "5" handshape touching the dominant side of the chest, flick the wrist forward, ending with the palm facing down.

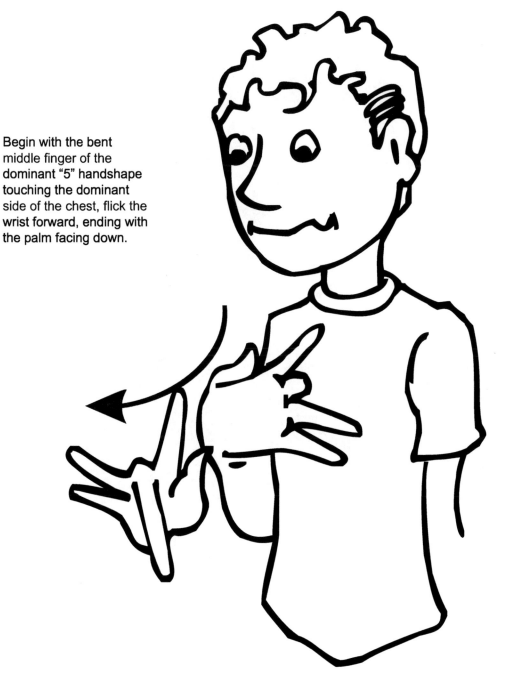

sensitive – sensible

Character

Slide the extended fingers of the dominant "H" handshape, palm facing reference, forward from the heel to the fingers of the upturned reference open hand.

[Also: honest, virtuous]

sincere/virtuous – sincero/virtuoso

Character

Slide the palm of the dominant open hand, palm facing down, from dominant to reference across the index finger side of the reference "S" handshape, palm facing dominant.

[Also: complete, full]

thorough – concienzudo

Character

Begin with both modified "X" handshapes in front of each side of the body, dominant hand forward of the reference hand and palms facing each other, move the hands forward and back with a repeated alternating movement. Then tap the back of the dominant flattened "O" handshape, palm facing up, with a double movement against the palm of the reference open hand, palm facing up.

[Sign: manage + money]

thrifty – económico, ahorrativo

Character

Begin with both open hands near each other in front of the forehead, palms angled toward each other, move the hands forward and outward away from each other.

[Also: open-minded]

tolerant – tolerante

Character

Move the dominant "X" handshape, palm facing reference, up and down with a double movement in front of the dominant side of the forehead.

wise - sabio

Emotions Signs

-

Senáles de Emotión

Character

Begin with both "S" handshapes in front of each side of the chest, spread the hands with a quick movement, forming "5" handshapes, palms facing in and fingers pointing toward each other.

[Also: frightened, panic, scared, terrified, timid]

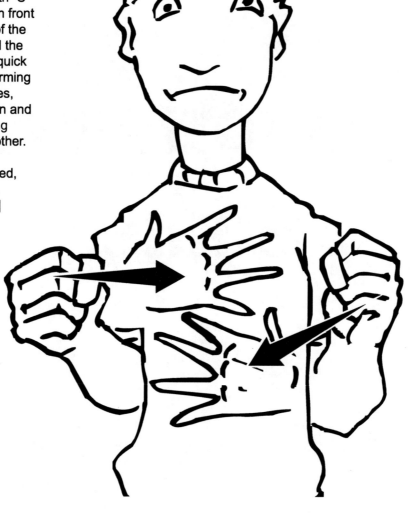

afraid - asustado

Character  73

Place the curved "5" handshapes against the waist and draw up against the sides of the body.

[As if anger is boiling up out of person]

[Also: wrath, mad]

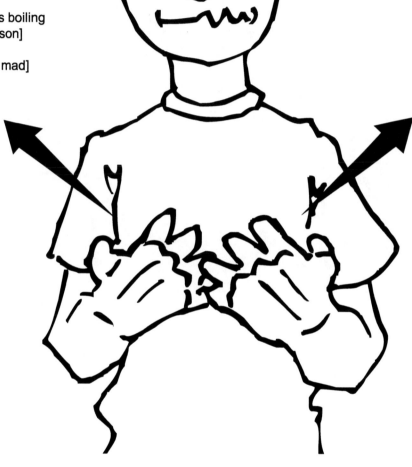

angry - enojado (a)

Copyright © 2008 Time to Sign, Inc.

74   **Character**

Place the tip of the dominant index finger against the side of the nose and twist the finger slightly.

[As if picking one's nose]

[Also: boring, dull, tedious]

bored - aburrido

Character

Move the extended dominant index-finger from touching the dominant side of the forehead, palm facing in, down to the front of the chest while changing into a curved "5" handshape. Then with the dominant curved "5" handshape over the reference curved "5" handshape, palms facing one another, move the hands repeatedly in opposite directions.

[Sign for think and mix]

confused - confundido

76  Character

Draw the index fingers down the cheeks from the eyes several times.

[Also: weep, tears]

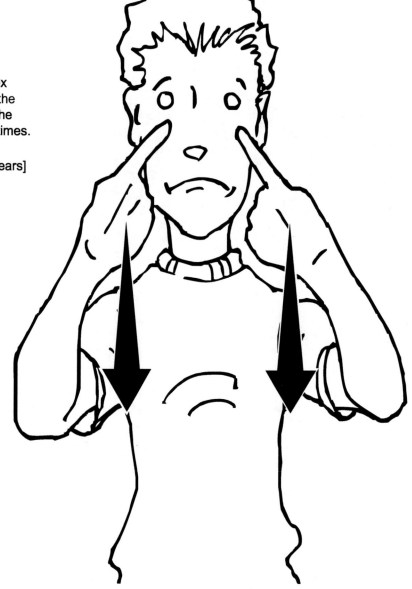

crying - llorar

Copyright © 2008 Time to Sign, Inc.

Character

Start with the bent middle fingers of both "5" handshapes near the shoulders, palms facing in and fingers pointing towards one another, move both hands downward to the waist simultaneously.

[Also: depressed]

discouraged – desanimado

Character

Move the extended middle fingers of both open "5" handshapes, palms facing in, in repeated alternating upward circles against the chest.

excited - entusiasmado

Character

Brush the extended middle finger of the dominant "5" handshape, palm facing in, up the middle of the chest with a repeated movement.

[Also: feel, sense]

feelings – sentemientos

Copyright © 2008 Time to Sign, Inc.

Character

Starting with both index fingers at each corner of the mouth, pull the index fingers down slightly while frowning.

frown – fruncir el ceño

Character

Move the back of the dominant "B" handshape, palm facing forward, up against the mouth with a double movement.

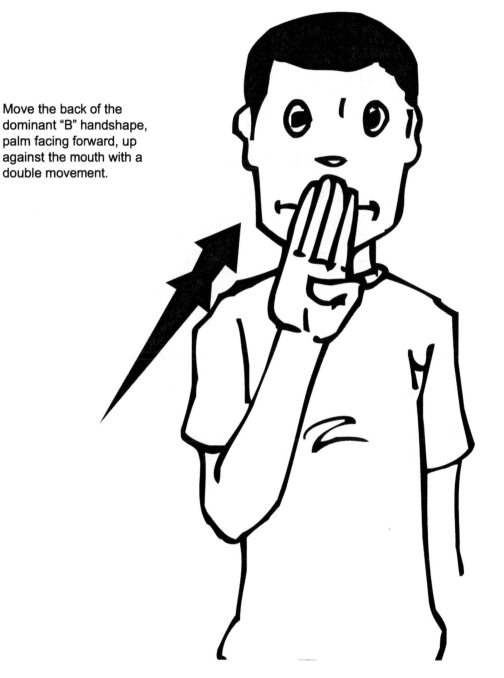

frustrated - frustrado

Character

Start with an open dominant "5" handshape in front the face, then move the hand forward while forming a "C" handshape, palm facing in.

[Also: cranky]

grumpy - refunfuñón

Character

With the open dominant hand pat the chest several times with a slight upward motion. Sign can also be done with both hands.

[As if heart is pounding with joy]

[Also: cheerful, glad, joy]

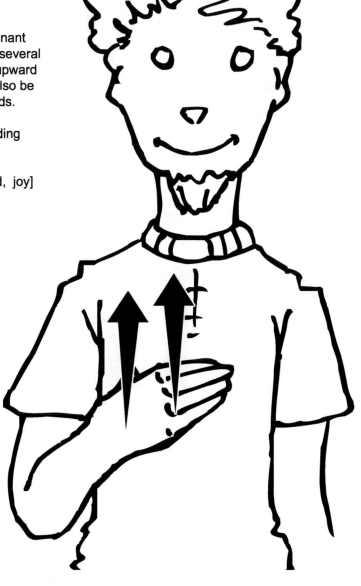

happy - alegre, feliz

Character

Begin with both extended index fingers pointing toward each other in front of the chest, palms facing in, jab the fingers toward each other with a short repeated movement.

[Also: pain, ache]

hurt - herido(a)

Character

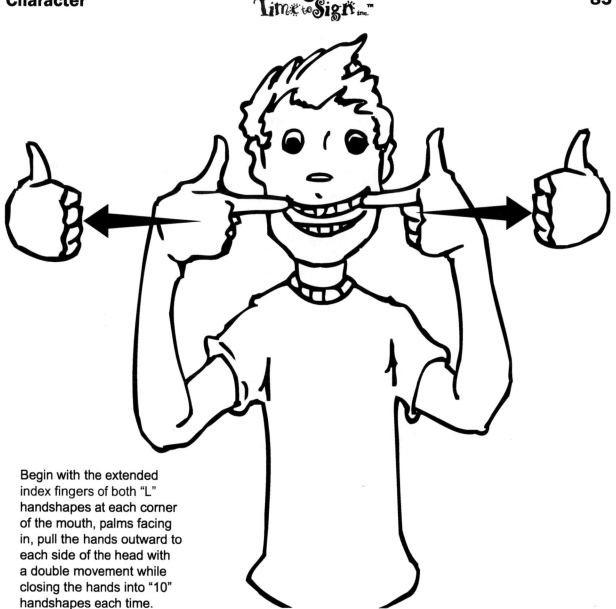

Begin with the extended index fingers of both "L" handshapes at each corner of the mouth, palms facing in, pull the hands outward to each side of the head with a double movement while closing the hands into "10" handshapes each time.

laugh – risa

Character

Place the thumb and the middle finger of the dominant hand against the chest, palm facing in, and draw them away from the body, closing the two fingers.

like - gusto

Character

Move the side of the extended dominant index-finger, palm facing reference, from near the nose downward slightly to just in front of the mouth.

[Also: lonesome]

lonely – solitario

Character

The "S" handshapes are crossed at the wrist and pressed to the heart, palms facing in.

[As if hugging one's self]

love - amor

Character

89

Move the dominant "M" handshape, palm facing in, upward on the chest with a repeated movement.

mood - humor

Character

Start with the extended dominant index-finger in front of the forehead, palm facing forward and finger angled up, move the dominant hand backwards to the forehead while changing the handshape to an "X" handshape.

[Also: perplexed]

puzzled - desconcertade

Character

Hold both open hands in front of the face, fingers slightly apart and pointing up; then drop both hands a short distance and bend the head slightly.

[Also: sorrowful]

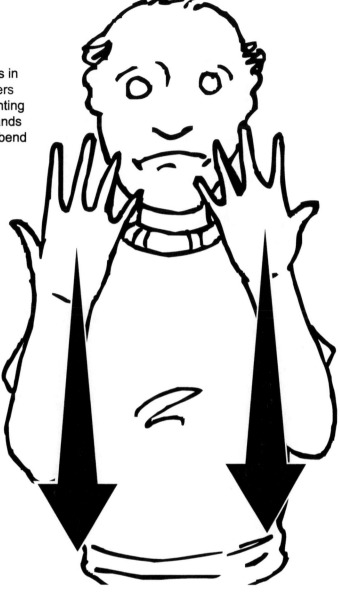

sad - triste

Character

Start with the thumb of the dominant "Y" handshape touching the nose, palm facing in, and twist the wrist outward in a double movement, brushing the nose slightly each time.

[Also: ridiculous]

silly – tonto, bobo, necio

Character

Start with the index fingers and thumbs of both hands pinched together above the cheeks, palms facing one another; flick the fingers apart, forming "L" handshapes near each side of the head.

[As if eyes widening with surprise]

[Also: amaze, startle]

surprised - sorprendido

Character

Begin with the fingertips of both bent hands on each side of the chest, palms facing in, roll the hands downward on the fingertips, ending with the little finger sides of both hands touching the chest, palms facing outward.

[Also: exhausted, fatigue, weary]

tired - cansado

Character

Beginning with the dominant "P" handshape in front of the abdomen, palm facing down, twist the wrist forward ending with the palm facing up.

[As if stomach is upset]

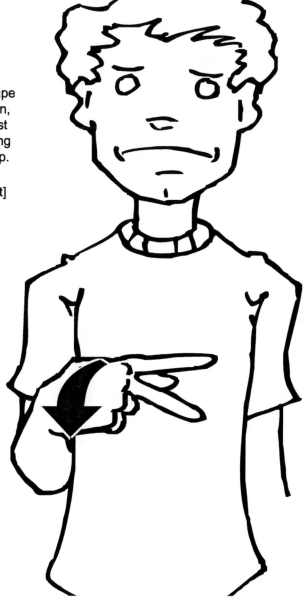

upset - disgustado

Character

Start with both "B" handshapes close to each side of the head, palms facing one another, brings the hands towards one another in an alternating movement, crossing the hands in front of the face each time.

[Also: anxious, concern, trouble]

worried - preocupado

Character

Greeting Signs

-

Señales De Saludo

Character

Begin with the thumb of the dominant "5" handshape touching the chest, palm facing reference, move the hand forward a short distance.

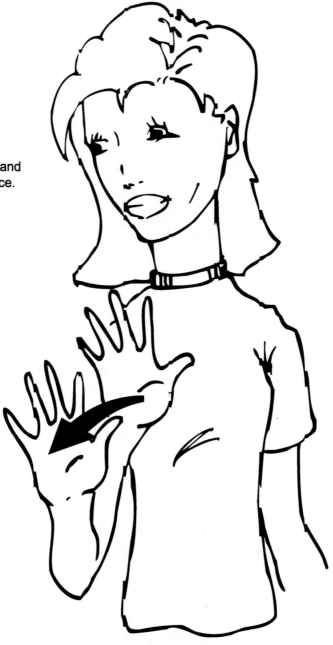

fine – bien

Character

Bring the dominant "5" handshape from the mouth down to the upward turned palm of the reference hand in front of the chest. Then with the reference palm in front of the body, palm facing down and fingers pointing to the dominant side, the dominant forearm, palm facing down, rests on the back of the reference hand so that the arm and hand point slightly upward, palm facing forward.

good afternoon – buenas tardes

Character

Bring the dominant "5" handshape from the mouth down to the upward turned palm of the reference hand in front of the chest. Then tap the heel of the dominant bent hand, palm facing forward, with a double movement against the thumb side of the reference open hand held across the chest, palm facing down.

good evening – buenas noches

Copyright © 2008 Time to Sign, Inc.

Character

Bring the dominant "5" handshape from the mouth down to the upward turned palm of the reference hand in front of the chest. Then with the reference open hand in the crook of the bent dominant arm, bring the dominant open handshapes upward, palm facing in.

good morning – buenos días

102  Character

Start with the dominant open hand straight in front of the body, palm facing forward and fingers pointing up, bend the fingers up and down in a repeated movement.

goodbye – adiós

Copyright © 2008 Time to Sign, Inc.

Character  103

Start with the fingertips of the dominant "B" handshapes near the side of the forehead, palm angled slightly forward, move the handshapes forward in a deliberate movement.

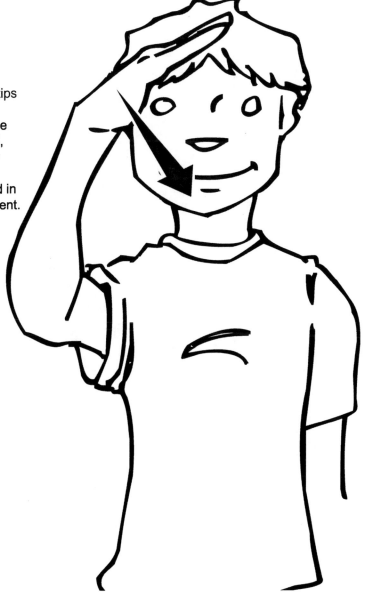

hello - hola

Copyright © 2008 Time to Sign, Inc.

Character

Beginning with the knuckles of both curved hands touching in front of the chest, palms facing down, twist the hands upward and forward, ending with the fingers together pointing up and the palms facing up. Then point the extended dominant index finger towards the person being referred to.

How are you? - ¿Cómo estás?

Character

Start with the extended index fingers of both hands pointing upwards in front of each respective shoulder, palms facing one another, move the hands together until they touch/meet.

[Also: greet]

meet – conocer

Form an "O" and then a "K" handshape in front of the dominant side of chest.

okay - bastante bien

Character

Manner Signs

-

Señales de Modales

Character

Brush the fingertips of the dominant open hand, palm facing down, across and off of the little finger side of the upturned reference hand.

excuse me - con permiso

Character

Starting with the fingertips of the open dominant hand on the lips, move the hand down to touch the open palm.

[As if something tasted good and you want more]

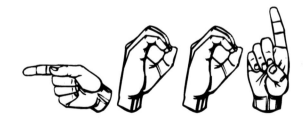

good – bueno

Character

Brush the thumb of the dominant "5" handshape, palm facing reference and fingers pointing up, upwards on the chest with a double movement.

[Also: courteous, polite]

manners - modales

Character  111

Start with both "S" handshapes in front of the chest, palms facing down, move both hands downwards simultaneously with a short double movement. Then point the extended index-finger of the dominant hand to the center of the chest.

May I? - ¿Puedo?, ¿Podria?

Copyright © 2008 Time to Sign, Inc.

Character

Bring the dominant index-finger, middle finger and thumb together in one motion.

no - no

Character

Rub the chest with the open dominant hand in a circular motion, palm facing in.

[As if rubbing your heart]

[Also: pleasure, enjoy]

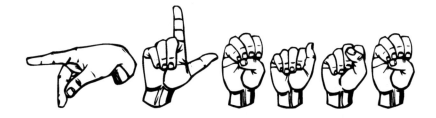

please – por favor

Character

Touch lips with the fingertips of the dominant open hand, then move the hand forward and down until the palm is facing up and towards the indicated person.

[Smile and nod head while doing this sign]

thank you - gracias

Character

Bring the upturned dominant curved hand from in front of the dominant side of the body in toward the center of the waist.

[Also: hire, invite]

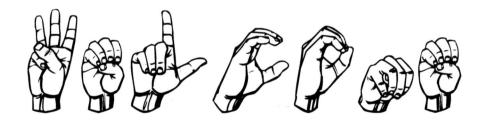

welcome - bienvenido

Character

Shake the dominant "S" handshape up and down in front of the dominant shoulder, palm facing forward.

[As if "nodding" your fist]

yes - sí

Character  117

SIGN LANGUAGE
HANDOUT – CHARACTER I

attentive - atento

compassionate - compasitvo

dependable - confiable

diligent - diligente

endure - soportar

forgiving - indulgente

Copyright © 2008 Time to Sign, Inc.

SIGN LANGUAGE
HANDOUT – CHARACTER II

grateful– agradecido

honorable - honorable

humble – humilde

loyal - leal

obedient - obediente

patient – paciente

Copyright © 2008 Time to Sign, Inc.

Character  119

SIGN LANGUAGE
HANDOUT – CHARACTER III

responsible - responsable

self-control - dominio

sensitive - sensible

thrifty - económico

tolerant - tolerante

sincere - sincero

Copyright © 2008 Time to Sign, Inc.

SIGN LANGUAGE
HANDOUT – EMOTIONS I

afraid - temeroso

angry - enojado(a)

confused - confundido

excited - entusiasmado

feelings - sentimientos

frustrated – frustrado

Character  121

SIGN LANGUAGE
HANDOUT – EMOTIONS II

happy - alegre

laugh - risa

love - amor

lonely - solitario

sad - triste

surprised - sorpendido

Copyright © 2008 Time to Sign, Inc.

SIGN LANGUAGE
HANDOUT – GREETINGS

hello - hola

goodbye - adiós

good morning - buenos días

How are you? - ¿Cómo estás?

fine - bien

okay – bastante bien

Character  123

SIGN LANGUAGE
HANDOUT – MANNERS

manners - modales

excuse me - con permiso

May I? - ¿Puedo?, ¿Podria?

please - por favor

thank you - gracias

welcome – bienvenido

Copyright © 2008 Time to Sign, Inc.

Index

A
afraid 72, 120
alert 25
angry 73, 120
attentive 26, 117
available 27

B
benevolent 28
bold 29
bored 74

C
cautious 30
compassionate 31, 117
confused 75, 120
content 32
cooperate 33
creative 34
crying 76

D
decisive 35
deferent 36
dependable 37, 117
Desire 51
determined 38
diligent 39, 117
discern 40
discouraged 77
discrete 30

E
endure 41, 117
enthusiastic 42
excited 78, 120
excuse me 108, 123

F
faithful 43
feelings 79, 120
fine 98, 122
flexible 44
forgiving 45, 117

frown 80
frustrated 81, 120

G
gentle 46
good 109
good afternoon 99
goodbye 102, 122
good evening 100
good morning 101, 122
grateful 47, 118
grumpy 82

H
happy 83, 121
hello 103, 122
honorable 48, 118
hospitable 49
How are you? 104, 122
humble 50, 118
hurt 84

I
initiative 51
Initiative 51

J
joyful 52
just 53

L
laughing 85, 121
like 86
lonely 87, 121
love 88, 121
loyal 54, 118

M
manners 110, 123
May I? 111
May I? 123
meek 50
meet 105
mood 89

Index

N

no 112

O

obedient 55, 118
okay 106, 122
orderly 56

P

Passion 51
patient 57, 118
persuasive 58
please 113, 123
punctual 59
puzzled 90

R

resourceful 60
respectful 61
responsible 62, 119

S

sad 91, 121
secure 63
self-control 64, 119
sensitive 65, 119
silly 92
sincere 66, 119
surprised 93, 121

T

thank you 114, 123
thorough 67
thrifty 68, 119
tired 94
tolerant 69, 119

U

upset 95

V

virtuous 66

W

Want 51
welcome 115, 123
wise 70
worried 96

Y

yes 116

Alphabet & Numbers Flashcards

These flashcards make learning American Sign Language fun and easy!

Learn the alphabet and numbers signs the fun way! These fun flashcards are made of sturdy cardstock, and are each 8.5" x 11" for easy viewing. The Animal Alphabet set (26 cards) includes signs for each letter of the alphabet, and also features animals pictures and signs. The Things That Go Numbers set (25 cards) includes signs from 1-20, 100, 1,000, 1 million, as well as dollars and cents, and teaches children modes of transportation signs as well. Both sets feature English, Spanish, and Sign, as well as brightly illustrated pictures and are laminated to 5mil thick to stand up to wear and tear.

Time to Sign inc

PO Box 33831
Indialantic, FL 32903
Phone 321.259.0976
www.timetosign.com

Contact us at 321.259.0976 or contact@timetosign.com for more information!

Time to Sign with Children DVD

10 topical signing areas, 17 songs, and 3 stories

Our most popular DVD, children learn to sign the fun way with Time to Sign founder Lillian Hubler and friends in this 53-minute video your children will want to watch over and over again!

Topics include the alphabet, numbers, greetings, family, manners, colors, animals, food, and utensils, as well as a section just for parents and teachers, Benefits of Signing with Children.

Songs include the ABCs Song; BINGO; Hands Can Count; Six Little Ducks; Three Little Monkeys; Please & Thank You; Apples & Bananas; Muffin Man; Itsy Bitsy Spider; Row, Row, Row Your Boat; Twinkle, Twinkle Little Star; Where is Thumbkin?; If You're Happy & You Know It; and many more!

Stories include Tea Please; Peek-A-Boo Pets; The Colorful Tiger

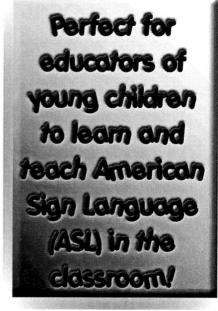

Perfect for educators of young children to learn and teach American Sign Language (ASL) in the classroom!

PO Box 33831
Indialantic, FL 32903
Phone 321.259.0976
www.timetosign.com

Contact us at 321.259.0976 or contact@timetosign.com for more information!

Classroom Materials

Our classroom materials help teach students and encourage further learning.

Time to Sign Pledge of Allegiance Poster
This 18" x 24" poster teaches children the nation's pledge in easy-to-follow sign!

Time to Sign Alphabet Wall Chart
Post this ASL alphabet on your wall to support children's learning. Features upper and lower case letters, the handshape for each letter, and a description of how to sign an example word.

Time to Sign Placemats
This set of 4 double-sided placemats feature the alphabet, animals, colors, family, numbers, school, and seasons signs. Placemats are treated with durable 5 mil thick, easy-to-clean plastic for use in eating and arts areas, or for posting on walls or glass. Over 120 signs in all!

Time to Sign Infants Small Placemat
This placemat features 18 common infant signs, such as mother, father, yes, no, please, thank you, bath, love, and milk. Placemats are treated with durable 5 mil thick, easy-to-clean plastic for use in eating and arts areas, or for posting on walls or glass.

Time to Sign, inc.

PO Box 33831
Indialantic, FL 32903
Phone 321.259.0976
www.timetosign.com

Contact us at 321.259.0976 or contact@timetosign.com for more information!